Facing and Fighting Through the Storm

by

Dr. Samuel V.A. Kisseadoo

RED LEAD PRESS
PITTSBURGH, PENNSYLVANIA 15222

The contents of this work including, but not limited to, the accuracy of events, people, and places depicted; opinions expressed; permission to use previously published materials included; and any advice given or actions advocated are solely the responsibility of the author, who assumes all liability for said work and indemnifies the publisher against any claims stemming from publication of the work.

All scripture references are from the New King James Version and a few from the New American Standard Version unless otherwise stated.

All Rights Reserved
Copyright © 2012 by Dr. Samuel V.A. Kisseadoo

No part of this book may be reproduced or transmitted, downloaded, distributed, reverse engineered, or stored in or introduced into any information storage and retrieval system, in any form or by any means, including photocopying and recording, whether electronic or mechanical, now known or hereinafter invented without permission in writing from the publisher.

Red Lead Press
701 Smithfield Street
Pittsburgh, PA 15222
Visit our website at *www.redleadbooks.com*

ISBN: 978-1-4349-6769-5
eISBN: 978-1-4349-2747-7

(PREPARING, ACCEPTING THE REALITY, AND DEALING EFFECTIVELY WITH SUDDEN ILLNESS OR TRAGEDY)

Dedication

My wife Henrietta and I wish to dedicate this book to the Medical Personnel of the Cardio-Thoracic Unit of Korle-Bu Teaching Hospital in Accra, and their medical counterparts of Komfo Anokye Teaching Hospital in Kumasi, Ghana, for the diligent, loving, and skillful efforts they demonstrated in the diagnosis and treatment of my illness, and the extra attention they paid to care for my wife Henrietta and I during my period of hospitalization and recovery. We also dedicate it to all of our friends, pastors, and family members who exhibited love and care in varieties of ways, and especially those who fervently prayed for us, in Ghana and overseas.

ACKNOWLEDGEMENTS

So many of you, very dear friends and family members, played significant and varieties of roles in loving, praying, supporting, visiting, calling, and being a blessing to us in ways that make it impossible to mention all of your names which will most likely cause us to leave some important names out. Two years after the events, we still discover great roles played in remarkable ways by many people in their secret closets, especially in the area of prayers for us that we never even knew about, and it will appear unfair to mention some names and leave your name out. We believe that more names of our behind-the-scenes prayer and loving heroes will surface as the years go by. We are extremely grateful to you all.

For the purpose of encouragement, however, please permit my wife Henrietta and I mention one or two representative names that typify what many of you did to demonstrate your love and support. We wish to express special thanks and tribute to Pastor Peter Shiltoncole (Senior Pastor of Empowered Christian Ministry at Ejisu, Ashanti, Ghana) who is the current Ashanti Region Coordinator of Fruitful Ministries International in Ghana. Pastor Peter was the primary person leading the Fruitful Ministry team along with me on the mission trip to the Northern sector of Ghana (Brong-Ahafo, Northern, and Upper East Regions). He handled my phone calls, stood by my bedside, and prayed for me through the night of my initial attack, refusing to even sit down, from 7 pm of Friday 24th July, 2009 until the morning of the next day and later run tiresome errands for us while I languished for a month in bed at the Komfo Anokye Teaching Hospital in Kumasi, Ghana.

We wish to express our profound gratitude to Dr. Ken Abboah and his wife Victoria Abboah who were miraculously used by the Lord to save me from untimely death by forcing to take me to the emergency room in the night when, unknowingly, I was a few hours from respiratory distress and death.

We owe much gratitude to Dr. Lawrence Sereboe and his skilled team of surgeons (Doctors Mark Tettey, Tamatey, Gyang etc.) at the National Cardio-Thoracic Center of Korle-Bu Teaching Hospital in Accra, Ghana, for the dedication, wisdom and tact they used to discover the root cause of my problem and devising an effective solution.

We are extremely grateful to the Staff Christian Fellowship of Kwame Nkrumah University of Science and Technology (KNUST) in Kumasi, Ghana, The Fruitful Women (a selected group of ladies I minister with in reaching out to meet the needs of girls and women), and leadership plus members of Fruitful Ministries International in Accra and Kumasi, as well as members of the Kumasi Ministers Fellowship, and several Pastors, church leaders, Evangelists, churches in Accra and Kumasi in Ghana and overseas, and countless Christian brethren inside and outside of Ghana, who engaged in aggressive prayers of faith for me and my family.

Dr. Abboah later teamed up with our senior Christian brethren at KNUST to organize special support in Kumasi along with some Pastors. Rev. Dr. Theophilus B. Dankwa and Rev. Osae-Addo (the former, and the present senior pastors of Accra Chapel) teamed up with Rev. Dr. Fred Deegbe (Secretary of the Christian Council of Ghana and senior pastor of Calvary Baptist Church in Accra) also organize similar support in Accra, and we are extremely grateful for their immense love and efforts.

We wish to express our deep appreciation to two Christian brothers, Mr. Virtue Addae and his friend Mr. Christian Bosso, who are Christian friends that were nurses at Komfo Anokye Hospital in Kumasi during my period of hospitalization. These two vibrant young men volunteered to give me a good bath everyday in the hospital at 6 am. They even allowed my wife to rest after her arrival, and continued to faithfully execute that loving duty. During the first week they even made time to bathe me twice daily. Two dedicated young men offered similar services along with the nurses when we were at the Korle-Bu Teaching Hospital in Accra. May the Lord bless and reward them and everyone for their loving sacrifices.

We wish to sincerely thank Mrs. Judith Agyemang, the General Manager of Kapital Radio in Kumasi at the time, and former Chair of the Ashanti Region Fruitful Ministries Committee in Ghana, who cooked and carried the meals to us at Komfo Anokye Hospital each day.

Our sincere thanks go to Mr. Ernest Commey who ran many errands for us in Accra, and was with us daily at the hospital. He teamed up with members of Joyful Way Incorporated (to which my wife, Mr. Commey, and I belong as old members) to arrange for six members of the group to volunteer and donate blood at Korle-Bu Hospital for my surgery on 26th August 2009.

Dr. Samuel Somuah, my dear friend and classmate from high school to the university level, played a significant role in transferring me from Kumasi to Accra for the major cause of my problem to be discovered and solved, and gave us initial care in his home with his wife Dr. Harriet Somuah during our first week of recovery.

Nana Abrah Adjei (Osiadan), our host in Accra, Capital City of Ghana, was among the first responders who traveled from Accra to see me in Kumasi (second largest city of Ghana) just when I was admitted to Komfo

Anokye Hospital in Kumasi. Nana and his wife Esther were always in touch with us until we were discharged to recover for three weeks in their home from where we departed to the USA.

PREFACE

In the evening of Wednesday 18th may 2011, my daughter was washing dishes while I was sitting at the dinner table, and as we discussed this manuscript that recounts my healing and deliverance testimony, and the fact that I almost departed to be with the Lord and face my Maker during the ordeal in July-August 2009, she turned, looked into my eyes and asked me: "Daddy, so were you ready to meet your Maker?" My answer was that I believe I will go to Heaven when I die, but if God kept me alive and was not ready to receive me at that time, then He knew I was not ready to meet Him yet; not because I was not saved by Jesus Christ or sure of my salvation, but because He knows that I have not finished my work on earth. God is very loving, but is equally very strict regarding his divine standards, and therefore He was also giving me the chance to ensure that my heart was completely right with Him, and to be certain that I have also completely "set my house in order" as He told King Hezekiah to do, when He sent him the message that He was about to take him out of the world. Meeting God is more than being saved. It also means completion of your earthly assignments and setting your house in order.

I wish to also ask you: "Are you READY to meet your Maker?"

"Many are the afflictions of the righteous, but the Lord delivers him out of them all. He guards (preserves) all his bones. Not one of them is broken" (Psalm 34:19, 20).
"But he knows the way that I take; When he has tested me, I shall come forth as gold" (Job 23:10).

On several occasions when I pondered on God's grace and His love that He demonstrated for countless people in the past, which was also manifested through people during my times of distress, especially the many faces that came across my mind who came around my hospital bed, I was moved to tears. Sometimes when it happened during the compilation of this manuscript, I was blinded by tears and could not see the screen of this computer that I am using. The song comes into mind: *"He washed my eyes with tears that I might see"*.

I encourage you to stay true to yourself and loyal to God through the darkness of your trials until your light breaks through. You are only "passing through the valley of the shadow of death" (Psalm 23: 4). Please don't speak and act as if you are building your home there in the valley of your trials and afflictions. By God's grace you will come through that dark valley victoriously into God's light on the other side.

"And it happened, when all our enemies heard of it (success in building the walls of Jerusalem), and all the nations around us saw these things, that they were very disheartened in their own eyes; for they perceived that this work was done by our God" (Nehemiah 6:16).

"Unless Your law had been my delight, I would have perished in my affliction" (Psalm 119: 92).

"Gracious is the Lord, and righteous; Yes, our God is merciful. The Lord preserves the simple; I was brought low, and He saved me. Return to your rest, O my soul, for the Lord has dealt bountifully with you. For you have delivered my soul from death, my eyes from tears, and my feet from falling. I will walk before the Lord in the land of the living" (Psalm 116: 5-9).

"The Lord redeems the soul of His servants; none of those that trust in Him shall be desolate" (Psalm 34:22).
"Before I was afflicted I went astray, but now I observe Thy word" (Psalm 119:67).
"It is good that I have been afflicted; that I might learn Thy statutes" (Psalm 119:71).

"Storms are **for a reason**, and also **for a season**. If you **discover the reason** you grow wiser. If you **outlast the season** you grow stronger."

Your waters can suddenly turn rough and turbulent. But, when your waters become rough, do not become rough in response. Sail across as carefully, wisely, and smoothly as you can, tapping into the faith, trust, peace, and gentleness that come from the fruit of God's Spirit, and the power of God that is released through prayer, meditation on God's word, hope, and obedience to God's will.

An unfortunate impression is given that when you are in God's will and serving the Lord with gladness, you should be free from storms and problems. That is far from correct. Jesus initiated a trip with His Disciples across a lake by telling them: *"Let us cross to the other side of the lake. And they launched out"* (Luke 8:22). The Disciples were right in the center of God's will, but a storm suddenly confronted them, threatening to capsize the boat and drown them. Jesus had fallen asleep as they sailed, so *"they came to Him and woke Him, saying 'Master, Master, we are perishing!' Then He arose and rebuked the wind and the raging of the water, and they ceased, and there was calm. But He said to them. 'Where is your faith?'"* (Luke 8: 24-25).

Storms are designed to suit each of us in particular circumstances, and are meant correct us and bring us back into the path of obedience, or to perfect us for stronger faith and deeper commitment. In all cases, storms prepare us for something deeper and important ahead of us. No one can predict in advance the exact time that you will be confronted with any particular kind of storm. But, when a storm suddenly erupts in your life, be wise, honest, bold, and humble enough to admit it. Then prayerfully gather courage to face that particular storm, and make a firm decision to fight your way through the storm, with a primary goal to come out victoriously, with God on your side.

Many people, who have heard my story in Ghana and overseas, interestingly tell me that I should write a book for many more people to benefit from my testimony. Majority of people say that God allowed the tragedy to happen in order to use the testimony to demonstrate His immense love and power, win people into God's Kingdom, understand the great things that God can do for His children, and ultimately glorify God's Mighty Name. I was convinced to do that, and the result is this book you are reading right now.

SUDDEN TRAGIC EVENTS — ONLY GOD KNOWS TOMORROW OR THE NEXT STEP

The year 2009 marked 40 years of ministry that the Lord started with me in the spring of 1969 in Secondary School in Ghana, West Africa. I was then 17 years old. That called for praise and thanks to Almighty God, and a time of celebration for what the Lord has done in me and through me. I, however, had a different kind of anniversary, and I "celebrated" it rather in an unexpected way on a hospital bed, including our 27th wedding anniversary that was celebrated 2 days after my surgery.

During my hospitalization, one Nursing Sister that I had known in her youthful days in Secondary School in Kumasi, Ghana, always made this statement to my wife and I during her visit: "We (Doctors and Nurses) give treatment for illnesses, but only God gives healing." That wise statement stuck in my mind, and I wish to recommend it to you as well. The timing of your healing and deliverance is arranged and executed by God alone.

Jesus said emphatically: *"Without me you can do nothing!"* (St. John 15:5).

You can never tell what can happen tomorrow; only God knows, because I left for my annual mission trip to Ghana on 20th June, 2009, intending to return on 19th August, 2009, but things turned out differently than I had planned, because of a sudden complex illness that resulted after an unfortunate incident.

What Happened?

I believe you are very curious to know what actually happened to me that triggered the writing of this book. The details are outlined in the chapters ahead of you, but in summary, the whole attack erupted in the afternoon of Friday 24th July at Tamale in the Northern Region of Ghana, in the middle of my programs in churches and schools, and conduction of seminars and counseling sessions as well as biological research in Ghana. Since my program was quite elaborate, many churches and schools were visited in nine cities of five regions in the country, and several seminars were conducted for pastors and church leaders and other groups. The itinerary had been completed for the Northern and Central sector of the country. I was completing the last set of assignments and move to the Southern sector to minister in three regions, when tragedy suddenly struck. Many people were also counseled before the enemy attacked for the rest of the programs to be halted. Our Fruitful Ministries team (Pastor Augustine Donkor, Ernest Commey, Kuma Gavu, Joyce Kusi, Alex Addae, Adokarley Opkoti-Paulo and others) were allowed by a few of the churches I would have visited, to conduct the meetings on my behalf. I was minding my own business when I had food poisoning which complicated into other things that nearly caused my final departure!

After spending one month in Intensive Care at Komfo Anokye Hospital in Kumasi, Ghana, and transferred to Accra, I was discharged from Korle-Bu Hospital for me to recover at home in the middle of September 2009, after 3.5 hours of surgery on August 26th 2009.

Sometimes I lay in bed wondering when it was all going to end, and asking myself: "How did I end up here to become such a prayer topic for the whole world like this?" I was careful about asking God "Why?" especially with a discouraging or doubtful spirit, which would dangerously seem as if I was questioning God's love, faithfulness, or integrity. I was aware that "Why?" is a question God would not usually answer in the heat of trials (unless He chooses to give you a hint), because even at the peak of His suffering on the Cross, when Jesus (in His real humanity) asked: "My God, My God, why has Thou forsaken Me?" No records indicate that God the Father answered Him.

If you prayerfully, patiently, and carefully analyze your situation in God's light and in His Presence (and especially ask Him what He wants you to do), then the Lord will drop ideas, directions, assurances, and answers into your spirit, and reveal things to you in varieties of ways. The Lord communicated truth to me in several ways, brought vital things to my attention, and taught me important lessons.

What Really Is Deliverance?

People often define and understand deliverance only in terms of "**being taken out of**" a critical, tragic, or destructive situation. But most of us either do not know or understand another aspect of deliverance which is "**being taken through**", in which case God allows you to go through the danger, trial, or suffering, but ensures that you finally come out victoriously. A typical example is that of Shadrach, Meshach, and Abednego (Daniel chapter 3) who were bound and plunged into a burning fiery furnace by King Nebuchadnezzar. God, however, miraculously broke their bonds for them to be free, but His Presence was with them in the fire as they walked about freely, still in the fiery furnace, until the King called them out to exit the furnace.

King David understood this truth when He said: "*Even though I walk through the valley of the shadow of death, I will fear no evil, for You (the Lord) are with me; Your rod and staff do comfort me*" (Psalm 23:4). David did not say "I will be taken out of evil at all cost."

People call me a living miracle of God's doing, because of the extraordinary way He sustained me and stopped me from passing away. When people tell me "We heard of your near-death experience", they are right. Dr. Barbara Entsuah (member of Joyful Way Associates to which my wife and I belong) told me on phone during my recovery in Ghana: "God was not ready to receive you yet!" Hmmm. That is a sobering thought.

Relax wherever you are, for us to walk through my story as I narrate as much as I can remember, in order to deduce important lessons for daily victorious living. I have included some thoughts on dealing with sudden storms in your life, healing of sicknesses, and purposes of trials. Enjoy reading the account, ponder on the rich lessons, and pass on the truthful messages.

"Extraordinary things happen to extraordinary people" — **Remark by Dr. Lawrence Sereboe who led the surgeons for my operation at the Korle-Bu Teaching Hospital in Accra, Ghana, on August 26th, 2009.**

TABLE OF CONTENTS

Page

Dedication v

Acknowledgements..vii

Preface..xi

Introduction...xix

Chapter One: Preparing For The Storm And Eruption Of The Storm 1

Chapter Two: Hoping And waiting Quietly At The KATH Intensive
Care Unit In Kumasi 17

Chapter Three: Transfer To Korle-Bu Teaching Hospital — Diagnosis
Of The Root Problem And The Solution.................................25

Chapter Four: The Importance Of Hospital Work And Hospital
Visitation 45

Chapter Five: The Importance Of Praying For One Another 52

Chapter Six: The value Of A Trusted, Dedicated, And Praying Wife,
and Love Of Family..60

Chapter Seven: Life Back In The USA 66

Chapter Eight: God's Way Of Healing..70

Chapter Nine: How Do You Deal With Storms? 79

Concluding Thoughts...82

Appendix 91

INTRODUCTION

REFLECTIONS ON THE STORM

My reflections begin with a search of my mind and heart for praiseworthy deeds of the Lord. When I do that, the events that I recall provoke sincere and profound thanksgiving to the Almighty God who has always kept me healthy since my childhood. During all of my visits to hospitals in my adult years, I have always checked "No" for the long list of diseases enumerated on forms that are given to me in doctor's offices to be filled before treatment. I have always been very thankful for God's mighty protection during my many travels across cities and countries over the past 42 years in ministry and for academic pursuits.

I was watching the Trinity Broadcasting Network (TBN), on 21st of December 2009, when Pastor Benny Hinn gave a testimony about his experiences with the accomplished televangelist Oral Roberts who had just passed away. He narrated how, at some point in his ministry, he was about to quit the preaching-evangelistic race because of the barrage of attacks that bombarded him, and the multiple problems he faced. After considering the issues for a while, he decided to go to Oral Roberts privately for counsel. Oral Roberts listened carefully to Benny Hinn as he listed all of his problems with explanation for each item. Then with a stern face, Benny stated that Oral Roberts looked into his eyes and bluntly told him: "If you quit, God will kill you! It is too late for you to quit now". Benny Hinn knew immediately that the warning was definitely from God, and resolved to stay in the Christian race according God's calling upon His life.

The Apostle Paul said: *"Woe is me if I do not preach the Gospel"* (1 Corinthians 9: 16). But, what does the 'Woe" really mean? It could refer to many things that could come upon a disobedient or disloyal child or servant of God who forsakes his or her first love and abandons his or her calling. The story of the prophet Jonah should always remind us that none of us can ever run away from God. It is often said that "winners don't quit, and quitters don't win." Let us learn to run to God and be blessed, rather than run away from God and unknowingly run away from the bright future He has designed for us, with a spirit of unwillingness to face the realities of life.

One of the most common statements of encouragement uttered by the majority of people who visited me during my illness in the hospital was: "It is well". I wondered why that three-letter phrase had become so popular from the lips of well-wishers to people in need. Up till now I have not asked anyone to provide me with an explanation for that popular jargon of hope and assurance. But I have paused to ponder on it and believe that it has its roots in the reference found in 1 Kings 4: 23-26 when the Shunammite woman's little son died but she still reported to her husband and the prophet Elisha "It is well" when asked how things were with her, despite the calamity that had befallen her. Later the prophet Elisha was used by God to bring the boy back to life.

A popular old hymn emphasizes the theme "When peace like a river attended my soul …. Thou has taught me to say it is well with my soul." Yes, IT IS WELL, no matter your circumstances, so far as you continue to obey God's word, abide in holiness, believe God's unfailing promises, trust His love and character, and place all of your hope in the Lord Jesus by beliveing His finished work on the Cross.

From time to time when incidents within the period of my ordeal come into my mind like video clips, I reflect on them and become filled with thanks giving to God. The reality of our frail mortal nature becomes very real to me, and my heart and mind become very humbled along with tears and brokenness. Today is 10th April 2011 as I pen down this portion of my story, and I was coming in the night from the kitchen where I went to drink some cold water during a break from work on my computer. After drinking the water I thought of my healed esophagus that was receiving the water and the different kinds of food I had eaten during the day. I thought of my trip in an ambulance for 170 miles from Kumasi (second largest city of Ghana) to Accra (the capital city) on September 22nd, 2009 when all hope seemed lost with no end in sight for my illness.

As I mused, God's love, mercy, healing, and grace dawned on me very heavily as I walked away. I paused, and suddenly knelt down spontaneously in the corridor leading to the staircase at home, and cried out in tears: "Thank you Lord! Thank you Jesus!" Everyone was asleep at home, and nobody saw or heard me. A familiar thought that I use a lot in my preaching and teaching came into my mind afterwards: "Character is who you are when no one is watching you."

The following is a statement made by my wife Mrs. Henrietta Kisseadoo to me (Samuel) in January 2011 during conversation at the breakfast table: "During your hospitalization in Komfo Anokye Teaching Hospital in Kumasi, Ghana, in August 2009, I remember the crucial times when I assisted the nurse on duty to push you in the wheelchair to the toilet room, as you sat and held your bottle full of viscous fluid from your chest attached to a chest tube. You used to look through the window of the toilet facility upstairs to count the number of communication towers in your distant view as an exercise to activate and calm down your mind, and get some feeling of the real world. During the week before we left Kumasi to Accra by ambulance for further medical investigations, you mentioned that your vision was becoming quite blurred, which we later learned were serious signs of your body fighting death inside of your being, as the condition approached a deteriorating point after which the situation would have been disastrous. At that time the actual cause of your illness had not been diagnosed, and no one really knew about the death trap within your digestive and respiratory systems that God Almighty, in His sovereign power, was holding in check. You had become extremely weak, and finding it very difficult to walk or even sit and arise from the toilet seat without gathering courage and strength by quoting the scriptures, typically *"I can do all things through Christ who strengthens me"* (Philippians 4:13).

Unknown to you, I looked through those windows as I waited for you to complete using the toilet facility, and asked God: "Lord, is this where you have allowed me to reach in life at this time? What next, dear God?" Every morning as I came to your ward at 6 am, I would pass through the male ward that led to your Intensive Care Unit, and would see 2-4 dead bodies wrapped and waiting to be moved to the mortuary. I would always look out for the type and color of the cloth around the corpse to see if it matched the cloth you had on you when I was leaving you in the night, and when I did not see your cloth, I hurried towards your room with a sigh of relief. God has been compassionate and faithful."

WHY, LORD?

When tragedy strikes or crisis crops up, the tendency is to look for explanations and answers. But God says: *"The secret things belong to the Lord our God, but those things which are revealed belong to us and to our children forever, that we may do all the words of this law"* (Deuteronomy 29: 29). Our minds are very finite, and we can know or understand very little. If God reveals anything to you, then that is great. It is meant for you to finally obey the Lord, so be encouraged to work joyfully and wisely with what you have at the moment, while you trust God that it will always be good enough and sufficient for your welfare, and for God's ultimate glory.

GOD IS SOVEREIGN

One thing we must know, understand, and be constantly aware of is the fact that God is sovereign in all of the affairs of men, no matter how much control we think we have over any situation that we face. God has given His children the mind of Christ for them to activate that mind through the study and application of God's word plus fervent prayers, in order to be in tune

xxi

with Him at all times, and sense the direction in which God is moving at a particular time, and move obediently along with the Lord for total victory.

"For 'who has known the mind of the Lord that he may instruct Him?' But we have the mind of Christ" (1 Corinthians 2: 16). The devil is simultaneously roaming around the world actively to destroy men and women plus everything good that he and his evil spirits of darkness can find and lay their hands on. God therefore ensures that His children become aware of what the devil is scheming to use as an attack on them in order to thwart God's plans.

"Lest Satan should take advantage of us; for we are not ignorant of his devices" (2 Corinthians 2: 11). God will, however, never allow any of His children to be touched by Satan or become affected by any evil without the permission of the Almighty God.

ZEAL WITH ENLIGHTENMENT

When attacks suddenly occur along the paths of life, they cause more wonder, amazement, and bewilderment when the situations crop up during an event or activity designed for the expansion of God's Kingdom, and to the glory of God.

In the past when I started being on fire for the Lord in my youthful days, I used to say that when I died one day, I wanted to die at the battle field of God, engaged in active service for Jesus. My zeal was so hot and sizzling, that I never stopped even for a minute to think of the implications of my statement, and to find out if God wanted me to speak that way.

Now I don't speak like that anymore, especially after marriage and having my own family that I need to take good care of and complete my family life assignments before I leave into glory. Also because there is so much to do for God's Kingdom that my focus is on doing as much as I can for as long as the Lord will allow me to exist and work together with Him.

I don't also speak that way anymore, especially after the horrific incidents and God's deliverance narrated in this book. I rather pray to the Lord to grant me extra grace to live and fulfill my destiny. Please be very careful of words that you allow your mouth to speak, because words were designed by God to be creative. *"Death and life are in the power of the tongue"* (Proverbs 18:21).

REASONS FOR ATTACKS, TRAGEDIES, AND SUFFERING

After experiencing a number of changes, trials, temptations, challenges, afflictions, and varieties of suffering in life, I have come to accept five major reasons or sources of these naturally unpleasant conditions, especially illnesses and physical attacks.

I wish to categorize them as trials and afflictions that we experience due to:

1) Natural or genetic inheritance from our parents that we have no control over, and for which we did nothing to bring it upon ourselves.

2) Attacks of the devil and satanic forces of darkness that operate in divers forms, such as occultism, witchcraft, spiritual transferences, or forces of oppression, possession, obsession, and depression, aimed at tempting you to weaken in faith and deny God. This was the case with Job who was attacked by Satan with boils all over his body after the tragic loss of everything he owned including his children (Job chapters 1 and 2).

3) Violation of a law (or laws) of nature, or careless living such as speeding that causes accidents and injuries when driving; unhealthy diet or unwholesome nutrition; unlawful or unwise and unhealthy practices and lifestyles that give you infection, body systems malfunction, mental problems, and other forms of physical ailments.

4) Sin, disobedience, or violation of scripture and God's laws that automatically cuts you off from intimate fellowship with God, dampens your joy and peace, snuffs out your love and zeal for things of God, or makes you lose your original anointing and God's hedge of protection, and thereby opens wide doors for spiritual and physical attacks.

5) Test, trial, or suffering allowed by God into your life to refine and strengthen you, test your loyalty, reveal your sincerity, and build up your faith to a higher level.

Attacks on the battlefield of the Gospel are common, because preaching the Gospel and teaching the truths of God's word to win and establish souls for the Lord are high level spiritual exercises aimed at confronting the devil and demons head on.

Even Paul the greatest Apostle had his share of confrontations with the enemy on several occasions, and once said to the Thessalonians: *"We wanted to come to you – even I, Paul, time and again — but Satan hindered us."* (1 Thessalonians 2:18).

MY SITUATION FITS WHICH CATEGORY??

Your thoughts, guesses, analyses, propositions, and conclusions for your peculiar situation could be as good (or twisted) as mine. In some instances, we can clearly discern the root cause, but in most cases I have to agree with you that it is very difficult to draw firm conclusions. Sometimes it even seems as if you are looking for a needle in a haystack. If you focus on the wonder, perplexity, and unanswered questions, you will become more frustrated and even depressed.

In my case, as well as for other countless distasteful occurrences, I can sense that you are seriously asking why God would allow such an excruciating tragedy or suffering to occur, and question why would God even allow trials and suffering in the life of His children, especially in active duty.

I need to emphasize again that apart from God using trials and suffering to humble, teach, train, strengthen, and bless us in His discipleship program, the Lord allows us to go through fire from time to time in order to ultimately refine us, burn away the works of the flesh, and make us more dependent on Him.

IMPORTANCE OF CORPORATE PRAYER BEFORE THE START OF MINISTRY

One of the lessons that I believe the Lord impressed strongly upon my mind and heart was the need to gather the ministry team members and engage them in more serious prayers of intercession before travelling with them for programs. Although each member was praying individually, such united prayer with me was lacking during some of the trips. I pray before leaving the USA to Ghana, and they pray before my arrival, sometimes even fasting along with the prayers, but it is important for all of us to pray together quite well after my arrival before we move out into the battlefield as a team.

At least three dangers will result from lack of serious corporate prayers by all participants before departure for any kind of ministry:

1) Poor preparation and coordination for plans and activities.
2) Team members will not properly catch the vision of the leader.
3) Lack of the required anointing and power of God for the work and its effectiveness.
4) Uncertainties about the required role of each member during ministerial activities.
5) Weak bond of unity, understanding, love, forgiveness, tolerance, and sharing among members of the team.
5) Exposure to satanic attacks, carnal temptations, and laxity, whereby participants will be lured into an attitude of being more of tourists and observers than committed ministers with a mission.

TESTIMONY

For the past 42 years, since 1969 when I was saved by the Lord Jesus and began preaching the Gospel, I have experienced several forms of spiritual confrontations, but in all cases God's love, mercy, grace, and power have been in operation to bring victory to the glory of God.

I wish to narrate one particular incident that came into my mind when I started to write this manuscript. Sometime ago in July 1978, when I was a biology teacher (and Head of the Science Department) at Tweneboa Kodua High School in Kumawu, Ashanti, Ghana, I was invited to speak at the Annual Ghana Scripture Union Rally for students on vacation in the Ashanti Region. The large gathering was at the auditorium of Kumasi Technical Institute, in Kumasi (second largest city in Ghana). I spoke for about 45 minutes, and challenged the audience to receive Christ as Savior and Lord if anyone was not yet a born again Believer. I also challenged every Believer present to re-examine his or her heart and life, and make fresh commitments to have a closer walk with Jesus.

In line with my usual methods employed for alter calls and prayers, I sang a solemn song interspersed with comments. Unlike many other occasions, I suddenly noticed a strange occurrence as my body began to sway in a manner that suggested I was going to fall down. Nothing in my being was abnormal, by the way – I breathed, talked, and felt very normal, except that a kind of force was literally pushing me from side to side. So I opened my eyes to find out what was happening. My immediate thought was that probably the large ceiling fan above me was producing enough draft of air that was strong enough to move my body sideways. That still sounded funny to me. I concluded that the fan was not responsible for the strange body motion, but forces of darkness were actively responsible.

It dawned on me that as I prayed for the crowd, evil spirits left individuals, in addition to demons that were always ready to attack any activity or move of God and children of God, and collectively attacked me as the leader of the spiritual activity. I therefore changed my standing position and stood more firmly with my legs apart for better stability.

After the meeting was over, I said to myself: "I am going to be in trouble, but God is in control!" I said so because for some time before that day, whenever I received intense spiritual attacks after ministry, I tended to have swellings at my joints that later disappeared after prayer, and I therefore sensed that something of that kind or some form of manifestation would occur later on.

I got home in the evening and lodged with my Kwame Nkrumah University of Science and Technology (KNUST) classmate Edward Opoku Mensah who was then an engineer with the Ghana Water and Sewerage Corporation, and was residing at their official bungalow in Kumasi. I did my usual Bible meditation and prayer for the night and slept soundly. At about 3:00 am I suddenly woke up and felt some itches at my elbow and knee joints. I quickly switched on the lights and saw large swellings at those joints! I exclaimed: "The thing has occurred!" My friend woke up and asked me what had happened. I explained to him the whole phenomenon and the spiritual implications.

Hearing God

So, what do you do under such circumstances? The first most important step during any attack or eruption of warfare is to get into prayer and ask God what is really happening, and what you should do. I did just that. The Lord directed me to read Isaiah chapter 40 and Psalm 91. May be someone reading this would ask: "How could you possibly know that God was talking to you?" The fact is that you hear God with your spirit, in addition to other signs and revelations or words and actions of other people and circumstances, all of which you should interpret in accordance with scripture, and how you sense things in your spirit. It means you must be right with God and in tune with His Spirit, have a focused expectation to hear God speak to you, and a burning desire to do God's will by obeying His word. Hearing God is a spiritual discipline that every Christian must pursue and practice until he or she become more familiar with the voice of God in his or her mind, heart, and spirit.

The peace of God in your heart, in addition to scripture, is the final test for God's will and God's voice. The information, directive, explanation, revelation, or instruction will heavily dawn on you and become infused into your inner being and engraved on your sanctified mind. Even when a vision, prophetic word, or word of knowledge, or special divine revelation is given exclusively to you, it is important that you ultimately test everything with the peace of Christ within your heart.

Victory Through Faith And Obedience

After receiving the divine directives, I immediately opened my Bible and began reading. I started with Isaiah chapter 40, and then continued with Psalm 91. I tried to ensure that my mind concentrated on the words I was reading in order to get the best meaning out of the valuable verses, and simultaneously build faith out of the scriptures as well. I finished all of my reading at 4 am (an hour later). I was then ready to bow my head to start praying but spontaneously glanced at my elbow and knees and saw no swellings at all! Wow! All had disappeared! Hallelujah!

That incident is one of the convincing factors that made me see a real manifestation of the power of God's word, to heal, deliver, rebuke forces of evil, and restore us to wholeness. I therefore praised and thanked the Lord rather than even asking God to heal me, and then slept soundly for the rest of the time. I have always agreed with Believers who emphasize that we suffer needless losses and pain because we do not understand and apply the word of God as God expects us to do.

These, and other similar occasions, are memorable times that God intervened to heal, rescue, and teach me valuable lessons of my Christian walk with the Lord. God continues to chasten teach, refine, and train me, and these will not cease until I finally close my eyes in death to meet the Lord face-to-face. God desires to walk and work with anyone who surrenders his or her life to the Lord Jesus for total control, refinement through trials and suffering, fellowship, and service, for that disciple of Christ to witness the same salvation, healing, deliverance, and assurance that God offers to all of His children to His glory.

Many Christians do not know or fully understand the value of suffering in the life of a child of God, as part of the great gifts God gives to all those who follow Christ in absolute commitment. Have you often heard it being said that: "No Cross no Crown"? Yes, that is absolutely true. You better believe it!

"For to you it has been granted on behalf of Christ, not only to believe in Him but also to suffer for His sake." (Philippians 1: 29).

CHAPTER ONE

PREPARATIONS FOR THE STORM
AND ERUPTION OF THE STORM

One favorite proverb of my late mother Margaret in the Twi language of Ghana (translated here) was: *"When you see or hear that someone's beard is on fire, you should fetch water and put it beside yours."*

No matter how a particular tragedy or trial seems enormous in your imagination, I believe that God prepares us for storms ahead of time before they hit us in life, although we might not be aware of such preparations.

Many of us know this truth, and we often hear people commenting on how they believe they had been conditioned and equipped to deal with particular problems they encountered in life.

RESPONSIBLE AND WISE PREPARATION

During the latter stages of my hospitalization, I had lost so many electrolytes from the abundant loss of fluid each day through the constant liquid effusion from my chest that depleted my electrolyte supplies, which had to be rectified through intravenous injections. We were sitting at the dinner table chatting at home in May 2011 when my wife Henrietta commented, when she saw me taking my vitamin supplements, that the idea of taking my daily vitamins and mineral supplements even on all of my outside trips, is a very good choice, because if I had not been constantly doing that "in preparation" for the problem I went through, my mineral and vitamin levels would have been so low in a short time that it would have created greater problems for me.

I used to also do some physical exercises at home and walked around the neighborhood, which gave me preparatory strength that helped my body when I had to lie down in bed on my back continuously for seven straight weeks. When I was discharged from the hospital I had to practice how to regain my walking abilities. In the recovery ward at Korle-Bu Teaching Hospital in Accra, Professor Rudolph Darko of the Ghana Medical School and then Head of the Surgical Unit at the hospital, who was among the surgeons that assisted in decisions and plans for my operation, visited me and told me to bend and straighten my knees rapidly for about 97 times each day as I lay in bed, in order to revive and maintain my muscle tone. I had lost so much muscle that my legs could not support my body for any long period of time. During the recovery period I remember squatting one day and remaining on the floor because I could not straighten my legs to get up.

My faith in God's word, prayer, positive attitude towards trials, good and balanced nutrition, and building of friendships over the years plus other factors collectively helped to sustain me through my ordeal. Since you never know what is ahead of you in life, you must make a firm decision to take every good aspect of life into serious consideration as you go through your routines. Taking a spare tire for the journey does not mean you don't have faith – it is rather wisdom. If you get a flat tire along the road (which no amount of prayer, faith, and good works can forever guarantee that you would never ever encounter it), then you will be in unnecessary trouble or need by refusing or neglecting to prepare wisely and adequately for the trip.

On 28th August 2007 when my wife and I celebrated our 25th wedding anniversary, we followed it up with a family vacation and celebration at Disney Land in Orlando, Florida. I did not tell anyone, but in my personal bag that I hang on my shoulders during the day, I had a little box that I filled with all the basic First Aid essentials that I collected from the medicine cabinet in our bathroom (cotton wool, antacid, eye lotion, antibiotic spray, Ben Gay skin balm, bandage, pain killers, spray for insect bites etc.). One afternoon after one of those speed rides, we were relaxing when the conversation of possible simple injury came up, and I brought out my improvised First Aid kit to show the family that I was ready to provide First Aid when it was necessary to do so. My daughter smiled and said: "Thank you Daddy!" I believe that all of these constitute part of the essential roles of a responsible father or family person — **Responsible preparation.**

NO ONE IS IMMUNED TO TRIALS AND SUFFERING

It is quite interesting that my sudden attack or tragedy occurred at the spiritual battlefield where all of us expect God to protect us and keep us safe without harm, because we are engaged in active duty and service for the Master. Moreover I had just finished conducting a Pastors and Church Leaders seminar where we prayed very well for ourselves, and was preparing for a family life town meeting for the city of Tamale where we had invited everyone to come for us to discuss marriage and family life, followed by a workshop the next morning after which we would leave for Kumasi.

Does it mean God did not care or was not powerful enough to protect me and prevent any tragedy? What about God's protection and provision for me since 1969 in travels through Ghana and other places like Nigeria, The

Netherlands, Belgium, Luxembourg, Wales, England, Scotland, Germany, Canada, and USA?

Unknown to people, anytime we are asked to thank God, or when I get into a mood of deep thanksgiving to God, one of my focal points of sincere gratitude to God is His protection and provision day and night in the air, on the sea, and on land across many places, some of which I refer to jokingly as "waterless places" that I traversed to minister especially when I was an undergraduate student traveling to cities, towns and villages and schools to preach and teach the Gospel of Jesus Christ. Almost all these were independent journeys that I undertook with no companion. In some instances, I told myself: "If you died here, who would even know that you are here at this time?" But God kept me.

God's love, compassion, mercy, and goodness are everlasting, and will never fail or cease, no matter what happens, and when it happens. God is, and will always be faithful, although I cannot always explain or understand his mysterious ways of accomplishing His purposes.

I have come to learn that **I cannot bribe God** with my ministerial efforts, services, sacrifices, offerings, and devotion. I owe nothing; He owns it all. Whatever I have and do is by His grace.

Yes, the Lord blesses devotion, service, and faithfulness, but you cannot give the full explanation for the reasons why some of His children are afflicted with illnesses and tragedies, or sit paralyzed in wheelchairs to minister; some struggle to marry or have children after they have done their best in life; many experience serious job and financial problems; and some wrote powerful hymns while they did so permanently lying on their back in bed; and many were tortured and even killed for their faith.

I believe that we need to say what Job said: "*I know that You can do everything, and that no purpose of Yours can be withheld from you. Therefore I have uttered what I did not understand, things too wonderful for me, which I did not know. I have heard of You by the hearing of the ear, but now my eye sees You, therefore I abhor myself, and repent in dust and ashes*" (Job 42:1-2, 5-6).

After we returned from Ghana to the USA in October 2009, my fist preaching in the USA was at Agape Life Ministries in Laurel, Maryland in August 2010. It happened that Agape Life Ministries, Christ Pentecostal Church, Church of the Living God, Revival Baptist Church, and Faith Family Ministries were among our faithful friends who interceded on our behalf in the Maryland – Northern Virginia area during the heat of events. I narrated a brief testimony to the Agape Life congregation about the unfortunate tragedy I encountered in July 2009, and how the Lord prevailed in the end and allowed me to survive the ordeal. After we returned to our home in Hampton, Virginia, I had a phone chat with an old Prempeh College (Kumasi, Ghana) school friend Kwasi Frempong and his wife Adwoa. Kwasi gave a very wise spiritual remark in his encouraging statements on the phone: "Is there anyone in the Bible we can mention whom God used but was never tried? No, we can't find one." He wanted to impress upon me the fact that trials are a vital part of God's syllabus for His school of discipleship, and constitute important divine training for every child He chooses to use for the expansion and establishing of His Kingdom.

In my opinion, the level and intensity of the trial is commensurate with your kind of calling and level of devotion, anointing, mission, and divine destiny for your life.

THE GHANA MISSION TRIP OF 2009

Arrival In Accra, Ghana

The program for the mission trip of summer 2009 was planned to last for approximately 2 months (22nd June to 18th August 2009). I was therefore halted in the middle of the activities. I arrived at the Kotoka International Airport in Accra in the morning of Friday 19th June with Delta Airlines that connected me through Kennedy Airport in New York City from Norfolk International Airport near our home in Hampton, Virginia. I was given the usual warm welcome from the Fruitful Ministries leadership and a bouquet of flowers at the airport, plus a great welcome at the home of my usual host.

Ministry In Accra-Tema Metropolis

My first sermon was on Father's Day (Sunday, June 21st, 2009) two days after my arrival, at Grace Baptist Church (Rev. Justifier Ocquaye), Sakumono, Tema. I spoke on the role of fathers in homes, marriages, and families. In the evening of that Sunday I gave my first live radio broadcast on JOY 99.7 FM in Accra at 8:30 pm for my regular weekly broadcast "Hope For Your Family" which can now be heard every Saturday morning at 5:30 am – 6:00 am on JOY 99.7 FM (the leading FM radio station in Ghana). The live broadcast can be accessed on the Web using MYJOYON-LINE.COM.

Before tragedy halted my mission, I joyfully and successfully ministered in 9 cities and 23 churches, and conducted our regular Fruitful Ministries 3-day Training Seminar for counselors and potential ministers to people especially regarding relationships, marriage, and family life. After completing ministry in a few other churches in Accra-Tema, I headed for Kumasi (second largest city of Ghana) on Thursday July 2nd 2009.

Ministry In Ashanti Region

The ministry team of Ashanti Region and Brong-Ahafo Region had gathered to welcome me on the premises of Kapital Radio in Kuamsi, led by

Mrs. Judith Agyemang, the General Manager of the station, and the Chair of Ashanti Region Fruitful Ministries at that time. My first preaching was on Sunday 5th July at Calvary Charismatic Church (CCC) of Rev. Ransford Obeng where we explored the seven pillars that constitute the ministry of every church. The Fruitful Ministries Annual Pastors and Church Leaders 3-day Seminar was successfully conducted for about 200 participants, followed by our Annual Women's Conference for the public which the Fruitful Women (selected group of women of God that ministered along with me) assisted me to conduct.

Ministry in churches and groups and to the public in Kumasi and surrounding cities went on delightfully, including town meetings on family life in the Ashanti Region towns of Agogo, Konongo, and Ejisu, and ministry to women of the Annual Ghana Baptist Pastors wives camp at Ejura, Ashanti. I spoke to the entire student body of Yaa Asantewa Girls High School on Saturday 11th July, 2009 about the importance of preparing for successful family life in holiness. It was a great time of interactions, questions, and answers. A similar lively meeting was conducted for the student body of Kumasi Girls High School on Wednesday 15th July, 2009, and for Kumasi Boys High School on Friday 17th July, 2009. In all places I had a very nice time of fellowship with the students and their teachers.

After preaching at the two morning services on Sunday 19th July, 2009 at New Tafo Baptist Church in Kumasi (Rev. Osei Mensa Sarpong), I set out for Brong-Ahafo, Northern, and Upper East Regions on our usual preaching tour in those areas with a ministry team of four and a driver, including the Ashanti Region Fruitful Ministries Coordinator, Pastor Peter Shiltoncole (Senior Pastor of Empowered Christian Church at Ejisu, Ashanti).

Ministry In Brong-Ahafo, Northern, And Upper East Regions

About 200 people from at least 23 churches in Sunyani and several ministers and town folk had gathered on Sunday evening of 19th July, 2009, waiting for us for teaching on marriage and family life at the Sunyani Branch of Calvary Charismatic Church (Rev. Roger Ohene Frempong), organized by Rev. James Appiah Kubi and his team of ministers in the city. The Brong-Ahafo Region Travelling Secretary of Ghana Scripture Union (Mr. Felix Annor Sekyi) had prepared the people with some good family life guidance to prepare the ground before our arrival.

A power-packed Pastors and Church Leaders seminar was conducted in Sunyani for 80 enthusiastic participants the next day, after which we proceeded to hold a Pastors and Church Leaders seminar and town meeting on family life at Techiman (Brong-Ahafo Region) for ministers, church leaders, and the town people.

On Thursday 23rd July 2011, we left Techiman at about 10:00 am and headed towards Bolgatanga in the Upper East Region. We made a brief stop-over at Tamale in the Northern Region to offload our luggage into our hotel (Mafara Hotel) since we would be returning in the night to lodge at the place.

We arrived at the Fountain Gate Chapel of Rev. Eastwood Anaba in Bolgatanga at 5:00pm. We had been scheduled to minister for 30 minutes on air at the local FM radio station and also announce our family life town meeting for the entire city that evening. After the radio program we conducted a two-hour well-attended and exciting family life seminar for the city of Bolga at Fountain Gate Chapel with Rev. Eastwood Anaba and his wife Rosemond present. After the meeting, Rev. and Mrs. Anaba entertained us with a delicious dinner and saw us off at 11pm. We jubilantly left Bolga for Tamale in the Northern Region.

First Attack

The first attack on us actually occurred at about 11:30 pm on Thursday 23rd July, 2009 as we rode smoothly to our destination. Interestingly, **I halted the conversation of my excited team sitting behind me about 15 minutes into our trip, and cautioned that we should spend some minutes in prayer after such a great ministry and accompanied joy, in order to thank God and ask Him to consolidate the fruits; and also pray for protection because the enemy would not be happy with us**. A short while after that we encountered dozens of cattle that had completely filled the highway. We could not spot the herdsman who was in charge of taking them out to feed at that time of the night, but our driver was driving at considerable speed, and had to employ all of his driving skills to finally stop at about three feet from the animals. It would have resulted in a serious accident.

We arrived in Tamale (Capital City of the Northern Region of Ghana) around 1:00 am, and rested for the night at Mafara Hotel. Tired as we were, we woke up quite later than expected, and had to skip breakfast, get ready quickly, and rush to be at the Pastors and Church Leaders Seminar that was scheduled to start at 9:00 am. It was conducted at the New Life Christian Center of Rev. Appiah Kubi, in the center of Tamale city which was at a very good location. The theme and materials were the same as the seminar for Pastors and Church Leaders in Kumasi: "Evangelism."

I spoke for about two hours to exhaust the topic as best as I could, and invited a few questions. We then broke into four groups for discussions based on the theme. In the middle of the discussions I felt the need to drink something, so I went downstairs to a nearby store and drank a bottle of 'Fanta' orange soda. I took the opportunity to witness to the store manager and other people around, and returned to the meeting room in the church sanctuary. The discussions were rounded off, and the various leaders gave brief summaries of the salient points and conclusions they arrived at in the small group discussions. I then distributed our usual Fruitful Ministries seminar certificates to all the participants, after which we closed in prayer and took a group photograph.

THE 'FATAL' MEAL AT THE RESTAURANT

After the Pastors and Church Leaders Seminar I discussed lunch with my ministry team, and they told me that our hotel could not provide us with lunch because the kitchen received the message for the meal preparation too late, but rather prepared to give us dinner. They then mentioned to me that they scouted around and found a good restaurant nearby, close to our hotel. We said good bye to the ministers and church leaders, and drove to the restaurant to have lunch. The time was then 2:45 pm on Friday 24th July, 2009.

At the restaurant we were seated by a steward and given the menu. The costs of the variety of dishes were quite higher than we expected, and we selected the local gelatinous corn meal "Banku" plus Okro (okra) soup (the usual accompaniment). After a short waiting period, the dish was served. I had an immediate negative reaction towards my dish when I saw considerable oil on the surface of the Okro soup — I tend to have more appetite and liking for non-oily that for oily foods. I therefore requested the waiter to take my Okro soup back to the kitchen and replace it with ground raw red pepper and grilled fish. It did not take him too long to bring me my new meal.

I started eating, but did not find the taste very appealing as the classic "Banku" corn meal that I usually enjoy. It was not very tasty as I expected. I also detected that a lot more cassava flour has been added to swell up the quantity and make it appear more glue-like than normal. Cassava is cheaper than corn, and adding cassava flour to corn meal for sale is a trick used by a number of traders and meal sellers. I could not therefore finish eating all of my food because I got bored with it after consuming about half of it.

When the waiter came around to bring us the bill, I remarked to him that they had deceitfully added a lot of cassava to the "Banku" meal to make more money, and should desist from such restaurant trickery. He gave me a broad smile and chuckled without a denial, implying that my finding and advice were correct and acceptable. He asked us if we wanted to order some dessert, and we answered in the negative. The rest of the team ate the "Banku" and the okro soup. We sat down to chat for about five minutes after everyone had finished eating, and I led the group in prayer to thank the Lord, after which we left for our vehicle to head towards our hotel.

MANIFESTATION OF THE ATTACK AND TRAGEDY

We sat in the car, and after I had I said a short prayer the vehicle moved. About three minutes later I began to feel a sudden churning in my stomach without any noticeable pain, but a slight feeling of nausea and sudden perspiration that surprisingly increased along with some dizziness within the next two minutes. I immediately alerted the diver to hurry up and get us to the hotel because I was beginning to have a stomach upset. The hotel was only 10 minutes away, so we got there after a short time.

When we arrived I rushed to the toilet to get myself refreshed, after which I felt quite better. The time was 4:15 pm, and I lay on the bed to get some rest for about an hour before the evening town meeting on family life for the city of Tamale that was scheduled to start at 7 pm. I woke up at 5:30 pm, and Pastor Peter Shiltoncole, our Ministry Coordinator, came around to ensure that I was up, and went back to his room. I felt a little sickly and the need to go to the bathroom. As I entered the toilet I suddenly started feeling very nauseous, and felt that saliva was rapidly accumulating in my mouth, with my stomach contents beginning to churn more vigorously. I was sitting on the toilet when I suddenly began to be extremely nauseous in a way that developed so intensely within about two minutes with saliva filling my mouth and material erupting from my stomach that churned so vigorously that I had no time to plan how to vomit, but quickly got up and turned into the toilet and vomited into it.

The vomiting process was so violent that I made very loud shrill noise as the contents of my stomach poured out. I did so twice in rapid succession. Immediately after that I felt incredibly sharp excruciating pain in my chest region that I had never felt before in my life! I wondered what it meant, and thought I had aspirated (some of the stomach contents had mistakenly entered my lung passageway). If that was the case, if I drank some water and waited for a while then things would get better. So I sat on the bed after realizing I could not stand still with the pain, then sipped some water and waited for about two minutes but realized that the pain was rather increasing.

I panicked a little, walked barefooted into the hallway and called out loudly: "Peter! Peter!" but the other members of the ministry team were further away on a different block down the hall, and no one could hear me.

People have asked me if I was frightened during the entire ordeal. It was that moment up till the time I was put on the hospital bed at the clinic in Tamale an hour later that constituted my real scaring moments.

HOSPITALIZED IN A CLINIC AT TAMALE, AND BREAKING THE NEWS TO MY WIFE

The severe chest pains intensified, and I began to grow very concerned about its source and implications. I began to feel strongly that I needed immediate medical attention. A nephew later told me: "It was a smart move you made at that moment to go to the hospital without delay otherwise it would have been fatal." Yes, God heals us supernaturally, but also uses medical Doctors, and has already provided wisdom and skill through medical personnel to assist us. God blesses the good medical efforts of hospitals and medical clinics to prevent and heal diseases, and save lives. True faith also applies wisdom, and effectively makes use of what God has already given to us for daily living.

Without wasting any further time, I put on my shirt and regular sandals (no time to even put on my shoes) and went down to tell the folk what was happening. I inquired from the hotel receptionist about the nearest hospital, and she told me that there was a clinic only a block away. I asked the driver to get me there very quickly which he did. When we arrived at the place, the Doctor on duty was attending to a patient, so I had to wait. After they took down my information I sat for about 6 minutes and felt the pain transmitting through my left hand. I was becoming restless and apprehensive, and entreated the doctor to hurry up and attend to me because I thought I was getting a heart attack!

After waiting for about 15 minutes, I was escorted to the Intensive Care Unit (ICU) that had two beds. I was asked to lie on the right bed, and data for my vital signs was recorded (temperature, blood pressure, and heart rate). Intravenous infusion (IV) was immediately administered to me, which remained on me throughout the night. I remember asking the nurse the constituents of the fluids at some points when an old depleted IV bags were being replaced with new fluid bags, especially when I saw him adding some chemicals. He explained to me on one occasion that I needed constant fluid in my system, and the chemical I saw him adding was Vitamin B. I asked him why I needed Vitamin B, and he further explained that I needed that for nutritional balance of my system that was having digestive problems, and to boost up my immune system. I was given pain medication to bring down the excruciating pains in my chest cavity, but the intense pain persisted for hours without subsiding.

Mrs. Judith Agyemang, our ministry Chair for Ashanti was not able to travel with us, and we called to inform her. She in turn called our ministry partner and my old schoolmate of Prempeh College (Kumasi, Ghana) Dr. Philip Opare-Sem of Komfo Anokye Teaching Hospital for advice. He responded in South Africa where he had travelled to do some work, a few days before, and suggested that it might be that aspiration occurred (food getting into my respiratory tract) when I vomited, so I should take some antacid and should not worry but wait for it to subside, ensuring that I do not take in any solids but only fluids. It was too late to receive the information because I had just finished eating bread and eggs plus some tea that the hospital gave me for dinner. Dr. Opare-Sem added that he would ask Dr. Ken Abboa (Head of the Surgical Unit of Komfo-Anokye Hospital in Kumasi, and also my old schoolmate of Prempeh College) to take care of me. If only I knew what had really happened to me, I would not have eaten anything at all!!

My Ministry Coordinator, Pastor Peter, asked me if we should inform my wife. After careful thought, I told him to hold on for us to get a better picture to give her. I did not know that she had already called to inquire about me. My wife later told people: "It was unusual not to have heard from my husband the whole day, because whenever he travels, he would call every morning and during the day, and especially in the evening before he leaves home or on the way to start the meetings. So I wondered why I had not heard from him the entire day."

Because we woke up late and rushed to the pastors' conference in the morning, I did not call my wife in the US, and the time when I would have called after the meeting was when the problems started.

When my wife called, Peter had told her that I was sleeping. So she said: "I am glad he is doing that, because he doesn't get enough rest on the mission field, so if he is sleeping then please let him rest." After she had not heard from me after three hours, she envisaged that I must have finished with the meeting, but had still not called, so she called again.

By then I realized I had to tell her what had happened, for her to start praying for me. So I mentioned to her that I have had some stomach upset and vomiting that appeared to be food poisoning of some kind, in my opinion. She immediately responded: "You sometimes surprise me. I have already cautioned you about what to eat when you are out there." I took it kindly and didn't see the need to defend myself and try to provide an explanation for this one, so all I did was to ask her to be praying for me.

I related to my wife the treatment being given to me, and mentioned also to her that whenever I lay on the right side of my body, I could not breathe properly, but could breathe better when I lay on my left. Peter advised me to lie on my stomach, and I refused it but tried and immediately changed over to lie on my back because it made no change to my breathing or discomfort problem.

My wife explained to me that it meant my left lung was not working properly, so lying on my right meant I was suppressing the good lung. **That was expert and timely advice from a loving and wise wife applying her nursing knowledge.** I followed her instructions throughout the night, and was able to breathe and sleep for a while.

When I looked at the time and realized it was 7:30 pm when I was expected to start speaking at the family life meeting, I asked Peter to call the Coordinator for our ministry in Tamale, Mr. Victor Tettey of the Methodist Church, and told him to inform the other Pastors to take over the Family Life Town Hall Meeting for Tamale city on my behalf, and inform the attendants to pray for me because I was indisposed and could not be present.

I actually had real deep sleep twice for a total of about three and a half hours between 10:30 pm and 12 midnight, and about 1 am to 3:00 am.

Whenever I slept and woke up, I saw Peter standing and staring at me, and trying to find out what was happening with me, and how I was feeling. He stood and communicated with me, and prayed for me throughout the night, and even refused to sit down on a chair nearby when I asked him to, except in a few instances. He was handling my phone calls to respond to those who knew what was happening and called to check on me.

The rest of my ministry team was in shock, tears, and prayers, and frequently called to find out my condition. Comfort, a young lady on the team, later mentioned to me that her shock and burden for my attack caused her latent asthma condition to suddenly erupt as she pleaded frantically with God for His intervention and my recovery. Peter asked them to remain in the hotel. Brother Faith (a school teacher on the team) in particular frequently called to check on me.

When my pains would not subside after the initial dose of analgesic (pain killer), I mentioned it to the nurse who explained that no extra pain drugs could be given until the correct amount of stipulated time had elapsed, since within the 9 hour period, I could take the pain medication only twice. I was therefore still in intense pain until about 4 am, when another administration of pain medication was given, which gave me some relief. I believe that the prayers that had been offered on my behalf contributed significantly to my relief as well.

I was subjected to abdominal scan at 4:00 am, and the doctor later came around to show and explain to me the images. He categorically told me that I had food poisoning when I ate at the restaurant, but they had dealt with the problem. He mentioned to me other findings regarding the state of my liver in particular.

I was visited by two female attendants from the Mafara Hotel at 5:30 am, and I witnessed and led one of them through the sinner's prayer to win her to Christ. I had already prayed to lead the other lady to dedicate her life to Christ the previous year. After returning to the US, I continued to be in touch with them by phone for follow-up.

At about 7 am, I was given breakfast of bread, tea, and eggs, which I was able to eat comfortably, after which I drank some water. If only I knew and understood what had really happened to me, I would not have done so, or eaten in the evening and the next day as well.

DISCHARGED AND READY FOR RETURN TRIP TO KUMASI

I rested at the ICU until 12 noon when the doctor told me that I could be discharged. The pain had come down considerably, and I felt a little sickly but was quite okay. I walked to the doctor's office where he gave me pain medication to take every 4 hours whenever I felt the pains in my chest. It was suppository to be administered through the anus, which implied I could not take my medicine in public! I asked him to change it and give me an oral version of it, but he said no, and explained that he would not do so because I had a digestive problem originally. I thank God he made it that way, now that I understand what was happening.

After paying my bill, I was discharged on Saturday afternoon of 25th July, 2009, and went back to the hotel at 1:00 pm with the ministry team that had come around to see how I was faring. I needed to rest a little, so I went to bed, and woke up two hours later. Looking at the time, it would take us 7 hours (without traffic hindrances) to get to Kumasi from Tamale, and besides, we would stop over at Techiman briefly (in the Brong-Ahafo Region), which would take another hour. I did not think it was wise to travel very late, so we arranged to spend one more night and leave the next day.

In the morning of Sunday 26th July I woke up at 7 am, and had my devotion, then had breakfast that was served to me in my room. I slept again for a few hours and got up at midday. We then prepared to leave for Kumasi. I asked the driver to buy me a soft pillow from town to lie on it for comfort, and adjust my position in a way that would offer more rest and alleviate the pain to some extent. That pillow was jealously kept, and was among the pillows used in my entire hospitalization and recuperation at home, and was brought to the USA as an object that is now cleaned and counted among my important memorabilia.

We left Tamale at about 2 pm, and had a nice uneventful ride to Techiman, 5 hours away in the Brong Ahafo Region. I had bought a large bottle of Lucozade energy drink that I sipped from time to time. Along the way at Nkoranza two Police officers stopped us and wanted to charge the driver for over-speeding, but when they saw the way I was talking with intermittent coughs and explaining my situation to them, the policeman remarked: "Why? Are you sick? Then why are you people not giving him any First Aid? Please hurry up and take him to the hospital!" I later learned that when the lungs are trying to expand, the process results in frequent cough symptoms.

On arrival in the home of Rev. and Mrs. Thomas Atta Akosa of the Methodist Church of Techiman, I secretly went to the bathroom to insert my anal pain medication. I realized that I was feeling a little weak and sickly, and they wanted to prepare soup for me but I declined with the explanation that I wanted to arrive in Kumasi as soon as possible. The whole family gathered around and prayed for me.

ARRIVAL IN KUMASI AND GOD'S MIRACULOUS RESCUE FROM SUDDEN DEATH

We finally arrived at the True Vine Hotel in Kumasi at about 9:30 pm on the 26th of July 2009. The rest of the team left me for their homes, and I went to my room. I read my Bible, said a short prayer, and threw myself in bed to sleep for the night at about 10 pm, with plans to go to Komfo Anokye Teaching Hospital in Kumasi for medical follow-up the next day, as suggested by my doctor at Tamale.

I did not want to be disturbed by phone calls as I slept, but somehow (by divine plan) left my phone on, while charging it at the same time. I did not fall asleep immediately but was pondering over all the events and meditating for a while.

Mysterious Phone Call From Dr. And Mrs. Abboa

About 10 minutes into my sleep, I received a phone call from Dr. Ken Abboah, (Head of the Surgical Unit of Komfo Anokye Hospital), and his wife Victoria (one of my ministry partners for the Women Conferences I organize, and leader of the Pentecost Professional Ladies group of the Church of Pentecost in Kuamsi). Rather than just asking how I was doing, and finding out what I planned to do next, they categorically told me that considering my circumstances, they wanted to come for me and attend to me in the Emergency Room of Komfo Anokye Teaching Hospital that night.

I explained to them that I had been seen and cared for considerably at a health clinic in Tamale, and was planning to follow up with a visit to Komfo Anokye Hospital the next morning. Dr. Abboa, however, still insisted to come for me. His wife Victoria in particular was more vocal, and irritated me with her statement: "Osofo (i.e. Pastor) you are very sick, from the reports we have received. Please allow us to take you to the hospital immediately." I vehemently told them I had already been in the hospital overnight in Tamale and had been attended to, and had been advised to visit the hospital for further check-up in Kumasi, so I planned to do so the next morning. I had taken my pain medication and was beginning to sleep, and was very reluctant to get up and go anywhere.

Dr. Abboa and his wife, however, ignored my protests (especially his wife Vic Abboa). I quite remember getting more irritated by the insistence of the wife in particular who kept telling me in the Ghanaian Twi language that from the description given, "Osofo. wo yare paa ooo" — i.e. "Pastor, you are really very ill"). I said in my mind: "Oh Lord! There we go again with these women! Unnecessarily being overemotional about nothing, as usual!"

Hei! Fellow men! Let us watch out! That is NOT always the case for the apparent impressions of nagging, complaints, expressions of fear, and insistence of women. **The women in our lives are special "radars", with great natural intuition and insight. They have been given to us by God to** become a blessing to men and families as warning bells! We need to pay attention and sift any wheat from the weeds (remember they are human too as we are with human weaknesses).

Dr. Abboah and his wife Vic still felt strongly to take me to the hospital that very moment, so they still persisted and came over, compelled me to get out of bed, and picked me to the Emergency Room of Komfo Anokye Teaching Hospital. **Little did I (or they) know that God was urging them to do so! Because I had only a few hours to live!**
Thick watery creamy fluid had filled almost the whole of my chest cavity, had collapsed my left lung, pushed my trachea, heart, and esophagus to the right side of my chest, and partially covered half of my right lung, getting ready to collapse that one too! I only had a few hours to get "drowned", sink into respiratory distress, and pass away in my sleep!!

Arrival At The Emergency Unit Of Komfo Anokye Teaching Hospital

We arrived at the Emergency Room of Komfo Anokye Teaching Hospital at about 10: 45 pm, and I was placed on a bed. My vital signs were taken (Temperature, Blood Pressure, Pulse, Oxygen saturation), and later on an X-ray of my chest was taken as well. Dr. Abboa realized my breathing wasn't smooth, so he asked them to give me oxygen immediately which they did.

Unknown to me, Dr. Betty Norman, who was the senior Doctor on duty that night, later told me that she had recognized me from a flier distributed in her church as the speaker for a Pastors and Church Leaders Seminar in Kumasi some weeks before, and she happened to still have that flier in her bag, so she took it out and checked the photo and identified me as definitely the person. She further said that after looking at the frightening X-ray film, she went into the room and told the technician to give her the correct X-ray of the patient under examination (i.e. me) because he seemed to have mistakenly given her some else's X-ray film. This is because the seriousness of the condition displayed on that X-ray film did not in any way fit the patient (me) lying down. The technician emphatically told her that it was my X-ray that he gave to her.

It was later that I understood why Dr. Norman, Dr. Abboa, and the medical personnel on duty came around me to ask me some pertinent questions such as: "Were you diagnosed of any respiratory or thoracic (chest) problems in the past? In what health condition were you when you left the US to Ghana last month? Have you had any health problems in the past two weeks, especially difficulty with breathing or digestion etc.?" I answered them that I was in very good health before I left the USA for Ghana, and had continued to feel healthy during all my meetings since my arrival a month earlier. Even on the day of the incident at Tamale, I had stood for four hours conducting the seminar for the pastors and church leaders without any respiratory problems or pains in my chest.

THE FRIGHTENING DISCOVERY! AND THE IMMEDIATE REMEDY

The medical team then briefed me on the frightening diagnosis revealed by the X-ray. They explained to me that thick fluid had completely filled the entire left portion of my chest cavity and collapsed my left lung, and had partially filled the right cavity of my chest cavity, and was about to collapse the right lung as well! That means "I would have no chance!" (as people often put it for those who encounter tragedies and have absolutely no chance of rescue or survival). In medical terminology, this kind of thick fluid accumulation from apparent infection is called "*empyema*". When I looked at the film I was absolutely stunned! My trachea (windpipe) and esophagus had all been shifted from their original positions to the right side of my neck region. **If I had continued sleeping, it would have taken me a few hours to get "drowned", sink into respiratory distress, and pass away in my sleep!!**

Dr. Ken Abboa explained to me that they had to immediately perform a surgical operation on me by boring a hole into my chest cavity, and insert a chest tube to drain out the fluid and free my lungs. Dr. Madonna Lawson assisted him to perform the procedure using local anesthesia. Surprisingly, within one minute, one liter of fluid filled the bottle attached to the tube! The liquid was thick and cream-colored. After the fluid had been discharged, another liter was obtained after three minutes of re-insertion. I was taken upstairs to the Intensive Care Unit (ICU) where another liter of fluid filled the tube after 30 minutes. I was given continual supply of intravenous (IV) saline and oxygen, and I rested for the night.

The next morning, Monday 27 July, 2009, the team of Physicians on duty, led by Dr. George Bedu-Addo, came around to examine me and ask me more questions. Others Doctors on the team included Dr. Mary Yeboah Afihene, Dr. Betty Norman, Dr. Afua Pokua, Dr. Salamatu Attah Lawson, and Dr. Kodwo Eyeson. Samples of the exuding fluid were taken and sent to medical laboratories in Kumasi and Accra for microbial investigations. There were even plans to send samples to South Africa for confirmed analysis of the microorganisms present, and the results to be received electronically.

The lab results came in two days later and indicated that the bacterium *Klebsiella* was found in the sample. From then on the best antibiotic for the group of organisms it belonged to was administered to get rid of the infection.

WIDESPREAD PRAYER, VISITS, AND SPECULATION BEGIN

As the news about my tragedy began to spread around, intensive intercessions were mounted for me in many churches in Ghana and localities around the world where people who knew me, heard about my predicament. I still had several churches to visit and minister in the cities of Accra, Koforidua, Akuse, Takoradi, and Tema, and information was sent to the pastors and leaders of these churches about my inability to fulfill those appointments. These churches therefore embarked upon intensive intercessory prayers for me. Announcements were also made on JOY 99.7 FM in Accra and on the sister station LUV 95.5 FM in Kumasi asking for prayers for my health and healing. Visitors began to stream into the hospital room to see me as the news about my illness spread further to many loved ones.

Several people (including some family members) are curious to know if someone deliberately wanted to poison me. The media almost made sensational news out of that! For example, a radio station in Kumasi wanted to make an announcement to report my condition, and called my assistant, Pastor Peter Shiltoncole, to confirm information they had received that someone poisoned me in Tamale. He had to refute and stop them.

So far as I know, there is no indication that someone intentionally wanted to poison me (unless there is a later discovery), but the most probable cause was toxin from bacterial contamination of the fish or red hot pepper that I requested to add to my "banku" (corn meal) and ate at the restaurant with my ministry team soon after we finished the Ministers and Church Leaders Seminar in Tamale.

Well, when forces of darkness are attacking you, they can use any tool or do anything to accomplish their goal — you can eat the best meal and sit in the best place and still receive nasty attacks. You only need to be extra careful, however, not to engage in any carelessness of any kind that will promote the wicked activities and schemes of physical and spiritual forces that work against you.

Mr. Edward Okyere, a former Travelling Secretary of Ghana Scripture Union, and present Leader of the Prayer Warriors Retreat team in Ghana (who led his people to engage in intensive intercessions for me) remarked to me during telephone conversation with him two years later after the incident: "We often play things into the hands of the enemy for him to execute his plans. The devil thought he was attacking you to destroy you, but now look at how he has rather opened the door for you to have a great testimony."

CHAPTER TWO

HOPING AND WAITING QUIETLY AT THE KATH INTENSIVE CARE UNIT IN KUMASI

"Through the Lord's mercies we are not consumed, because His compassions fail not. They are new every morning; Great is Your faithfulness. The Lord is my portion, says my soul, therefore I hope in Him! The Lord is good to those who wait for Him. It is good that one should hope and wait quietly for the salvation of the Lord" (Lamentations 3: 22-26).

LIFE AT KOMFO ANOKYE TEACHING HOSPITAL (KATH), KUMASI

Until the arrival of this tragedy and accompanying episode, I had had no hospitalization experience in my life. When I was an undergraduate and later graduate student at the Kwame Nkrumah University of Science and Technology (KNUST) in Kumasi, Ghana, I was known as "the student evangelist" who ran around many Secondary Schools and university campuses as well as Training Colleges and some churches preaching the Gospel.

I hated to think that I would be hospitalized one day and miss any preaching appointment, and I therefore firmly declared that I would never be so sick as to merit admission at any hospital or clinic. My faith and prediction came to pass perfectly, and I was never admitted into any hospital from 1973 to 1977 (as an undergraduate) or 1979 to 1982 (as a graduate student).

I frequently emphasized, to many loved ones and well-wishers who visited me at the KATH ICU, how surprised I was about my hospitalization. I remember saying on more than one occasion: "I have never been admitted to sleep on any hospital bed before in my life. Now I have to experience it for the first time, and here I am lying on a hospital bed for days on end!"

I am sure that someone reading this will definitely identify with me. You wonder why your life could change so suddenly in a moment, unannounced, and you are thereby tempted to ask many questions that seem to have no answers.

On many occasions I exhorted people who visited me, especially at the beginning of my hospitalization, to be humble, stop grumbling and complaining, especially about personal preferences. I exhorted them to learn the art of forgiveness, and live with the constant thought that we do not by any right deserve anything good in life because of any special virtue any of us possesses or because of any accomplishment — everything is a gift from God, and all that we have is provided by God's grace.

BENEFITS OF REST, REFLECTION, AND REJUVENATION

No matter the situation or explanation, we need to accept the fact that God uses trying times to provide us with proper focused attention on our own needs, extended times of reflection on our lives, plus much-needed physical and mental rest, as we meditate in God's Presence. On such occasions we realize that we are literally grounded, and are compelled to stop moving around and stay at home to rest.

Before I even heard some comments from people that confirmed my thoughts regarding my situation, I deeply sensed that many would think I had fallen ill through body fatigue. One beloved Christian friend who heard about my illness, and called to check on me in the hospital, immediately remarked: "Uncle (as he and his wife plus some close friends affectionately called me) your program! Your preaching itinerary is typically crammed with too many activities without any rest!"

Almost everyone who heard that I had been hospitalized drew an immediate conclusion that I had "burned out" and broken down from physical stress and fatigue. But, that was not the case. I learned that it is always best and appropriate to patiently wait to obtain all the facts before arriving at definite conclusions especially for unexpected events.

Even after learning of the real cause of my hospitalization, many persons still felt that it was, indirectly, a good time of rest for me, from busy teaching, evangelistic, and other activities. One Nursing Sister at KATH who is a beloved old time daughter in the Lord that I knew from her secondary school in the 1970's visited me from time to time and remarked: "We don't want to say that he is really sick at this time, but God is giving him some time to rest, because this body of his would not normally get enough rest."

In this instance a different diagnosis had been made that was far removed from any breakdown of my body, but was inconclusive, and which somehow baffled the doctors to some extent. The day after my hospitalization my wife (who is a nurse and therefore has medical experience) called during the mid-morning hours to find out from the doctors and nurses what was really wrong with her husband. I saw that the leading medical officer in charge, who happened to be around, was reluctant to talk to her on the phone, and actually did not take the call when Peter (my assistant) tried to hand the phone to him. What I heard him say was: "How can I tell her what is wrong with her husband when I don't really know what is going on with him?"

DEATH AND LIFE AROUND ME

I saw instances on the wards when some people recovered or improved and were happily sent home. I, however, recount deaths almost every morning at the regular male ward next door, and lamentations of loved ones during my bathing time around 6:00 am. The first time I heard such loud shouting, crying, and stamping of feet I asked Virtue (one of the brothers who voluntarily cleaned me) what it meant, and he explained that the commotion signaled the death of a loved. When relatives came early morning and did not find their loved one in his or her bed, and were told that the one passed away in the night for the body to be removed to the mortuary, the shock erupted into desperate cries and production of noise from different motions of feet and hands.

I remember a Japanese man who had come into the country on an assignment but suddenly had a heart attack and was brought into the ICU one afternoon. He slept opposite me, and was in intense pain. Around 1:00 am the next morning, he made a loud noise with his throat, and the two nurses on duty went to his aid. Seeing the seriousness of the situation, they called for the doctor on duty who examined him and found him suddenly dead, with no chance to revive him. Shortly later his body was carried out. All these taught me the lessons of the shortness of human life, but did not really frighten me to expect the worst.

TRYING TO RESOLVE THE PUZZLE, AND INITIAL CARE

The team of Doctors came round every morning for their usual medical rounds. Led by their senior medical doctor, pertinent questions were asked, my medical chart information was examined, and drug recommendations were consequently determined.

The focus was on destroying the microbes that caused the infection in my chest region, which was pursued with the best antibiotics that were most effective against the suspected and confirmed microorganisms. When doctors wrote prescriptions, Peter (my ministry assistant) who did most of the errands, was directed to buy the drugs at specific trusted pharmacy stores. Several fake and counterfeit drugs were floating around many pharmacy shops in the cities and towns, and the practice still continues which causes unnecessary deaths of patients with simple malaria and other ailments that should not result in death of the victims.

Different combinations of pain medications were given to me at prescribed times, and sometimes when I felt intense pain after the effects of the drug wore out, I wanted some medicine for relief which was refused until the correct time interval had been observed. I found morphine to be the best to subside my pain, for me to have tremendous relief for a few hours, but they did not want me to become dependent on it since it could become addictive, and also has the side effect of repressing the respiratory system. High or frequent doses of morphine were not was therefore very appropriate for a patient whose lung had collapsed and was being treated to have normal respiration again. My wife in particular, who employed her nursing knowledge to care for me, was strict on me regarding my constant demand for morphine. Most often when I was alone with the night nurse, I would bother her deep in the night to give me morphine when my pain grew intense because the effects of the previous medication had worn down.

To reactivate and rehabilitate my lungs, balloons were given to me to blow air into them frequently each day. I also had a respiratory instrument (spirometer) my wife carried with her from the USA that I blew air through to improve my lung functioning, and which also measured my lung capacity.

I could eat normally, and food was ordered for me from the hospital kitchen. One doctor who knew me and was in touch with the kitchen came up to tell me he had specially instructed that my soup and stew should be fortified with fresh local *Solanum torvum* variety (member of the plant family Solanacea —the eggplant family) that is reputed to be highly anti-hypertensive and very nutritious.

After my wife arrived from the USA, my food was specially prepared by Mrs. Judith Agyemang, then General Manager of Kapital Radio and Ashanti Region Chair of our ministry (Fruitful Ministries International Inc.). She came in the morning to visit with breakfast, and came with lunch as well. She came with my dinner and would ask me what I desired to eat for the next day. In a few instances when she had other things to do, she sent the food through her secretary Helen Amponsah, or her driver Solomon.

AGGRAVATION OF MY CONDITION

As the days progressed, the veins on the periphery of my body collapsed, and it was a real tug-of-war for the nurses and doctors to get my vein for the drawing of blood and other medical procedures. All of my veins had virtually collapsed as a sign of my heart not pumping enough blood to reach the surface of my body. In some cases a number of tries were made to get a vein but all attempts proved futile. On one occasion a doctor spent a long time trying to get a vein to insert a needle and used all the methods he could employ but pierced me three times without success and left in frustration, so an expert had to be called in to massage my hand with warm water and use special anatomical and surgical skills to get into a major vein for an intravenous procedure.

I later joked that my arms had so many piercings and 'thrombosed' (blocked) dark veins that if I went for a job interview soon after being discharged, I would be driven away due to the suspicion of being a drug pusher and user.

As I mentioned, only morphine could subdue the pain enough as my condition worsened, especially for me to get some good sleep at night. My wife Henrietta used to get concerned over that, because morphine has the side effect of suppressing the respiratory system, and with my body being so weak, she was apprehensive that I might be put to sleep by morphine and fall into a coma.

During the latter stages of my stay in the Komfo Anokye ICU, I experienced very cold extremities of my toes and fingers. I remember one night when I called for the attention of the Cover Doctor (the doctor on duty) when I was experiencing breathing and sleeping difficulties. As he examined me he remarked: "Your fingers and toes are really very cold!" Later I learned that my body was desperately fighting to keep me alive such that blood was being directed to the major areas within my main body, resulting in cold fingers and toes, and which also collapsed superficial veins. All these were dangerous signs of progression towards cessation of body functions and possible death.

I began to feel weaker with passing time, and felt more pains too in my body especially my chest region. I felt an exclusive sharp pain in my sternum area (middle of my chest) and mentioned it to my doctors, but I did not know how that was interpreted. I recall telling them one afternoon: "I feel a strange burning pain around my sternum (breastbone)." No real response was given to my complaint, and it appeared dismissed.

In the latter stages of my hospitalization in Kumasi, the pains were so excruciating when I sat to eat, such that I focused more on the pain than on the food, and could not enjoy the meals. I was therefore being fed in bed by my wife, and sometimes by our friend Judith.

I remember asking for fresh soft coconut which was brought to me one afternoon. When I began to consume the mixture of the coconut flesh and the water, I felt a very sharp unbearable pain in the center of my chest and began to scream, which was quite strange because other food items I ate did not give me such intense pain. Oranges gave me a little more pain than normal, but did not match the coconut pain level. When I ate the coconut flesh alone, the very sharp pain subsided very significantly. When I drank the coconut juice, I had to scream to express my pain. Later on when the real diagnosis came out to reveal what had happened to my digestive tract, then I understood why I experienced all that pain in my body.

During that period I began sweating very profusely after the first week. Big blobs of sweat covered my body especially my face and chest areas. I could sweat to such an extent that my entire clothing and pillow plus bed sheet were soaked in sweat even when the weather was cold. I always had towels to wipe the sweat, and my wife had to often change my sweat-soaked clothing. A nurse remarked one afternoon: "Doctor, you are sweating so much even when it is cold." I later came to learn that the profuse sweating was one of the major signs that my body was fighting desperately to keep me alive.

I began to feel very weak after the first three weeks, which grew worse during the last week before I was taken to Accra (Capital City of Ghana), and could not walk with assistance to the toilet anymore without being carried in a wheelchair to and fro. When I sat on the toilet, getting up was a tug of war, and on several occasions I gathered courage and quoted scriptures like: "*I can do all things through Christ who strengthens me*" (Philippians 4:13) before I could stand up. I even quoted inspirational scriptures on the way to the toilet.

From the toilet facility on the fourth floor of the hospital I could see some parts of Kumasi city through the window, which gave me my only outside view for the day except when I was wheeled across to the next block for X-rays that gave me some glimpse and momentary interaction with the outside world.

I noticed that during my latter days in Kumasi, my vision started getting blurry, even when I put on my glasses, and I thought it was due to the many hospital chemicals (medications) I had taken into my body. Although that was a factor, I could not fully understand the condition, but later when my real diagnosis was made, my wife used her nursing skills to explain to me that she saw me deteriorating as the days went by, and realized that I was slowly becoming more dehydrated and gradually dying if conditions did not change. My body was indeed struggling through the shock and massive infection plus respiratory complications to still keep me alive, backed, of course, by God's mighty Hand at the background. My body was beginning to get tired of fighting to keep me alive, but I believe God would have still kept me going, and He allowed me to leave for Accra at that crucial time for further medical intervention.

I noticed that growth ceased in my body. The hair on my head and my finger nails stopped growing. My infectious disease specialist in the USA explained to me that my body was so shocked that normal processes of growth suddenly stopped. I had what is called "Beau's Lines" across my finger nails that were definite white lines that divided the old growth from the new growth when I began to recover. After a few months when the body resumed normal growth, my finger nails grew and finally pushed the lines upwards and finally out of view.

THE VALUE OF GOD'S WORD AND PERSONAL PRAYER IN THE MIDST OF TRIALS AND SUFFERING

As I look back I can see the working of the mighty power of God and His comfort plus grace for His children in all matters and situations of life. As frightening and disturbing as my condition was, the Lord enabled me to remain calm and mostly cheerful throughout those crucial periods without even shedding a tear once, except one or two occasions when I wept briefly in private prayer, which was more of repentance and brokenness before the Lord when I became more aware of the frailty and weakness of mortal humans, and the need to develop humble hearts at all times.

The Presence of God's Holy Spirit, daily word of God from the scriptures, prayer, constant love and care of beloved ones, words of encouragement from visitors and callers, provision of God's grace and mercy, and the hope in God's character and His good deeds of the past plus His unfailing promises, were the primary tools that sustained me through the ordeal.

The sickly feeling in my body and mixed emotions largely caused me not to experience the deep 'normal anointed and sensational feeling' (as I may put it) that I regularly felt during prayers, but the joy of the Lord was deep in the background of my heart and spirit, and I still enjoyed my prayers and believed that God heard every word from my lips and heart. **I learned to walk by faith more than by sight and feelings** (2 Corinthians 5:7).

Sometimes I prayed and expected immediate or quick elimination of some pains or cessation of the fluid from my chest but I did not get immediate results. Several hours or even days later I saw improvement especially with the pain.

The experiences reminded me of the way faith works, and made me learn more of the cumulative effects of our faith and prayers, as well as the timing of God's responses to our prayers, emphasizing the fact that God answers prayers and works according to His own timing.

I strengthened my spirit a lot with scripture during my hospitalization. Every morning before 6am I would take my Bible to read and meditate on some verses, and pray before my nurses came around to give me a bath. I did not only focus on verses for healing and answers to prayer, but focused also on scriptures that encouraged changes and building of godly character in me.

Some of the scriptures I particularly recited and depended on were verses like *"By His (Jesus) stripes we were healed"* (1 Peter 2:24). My wife reminded me later that I used Psalm 27:13 a lot for prayer in Kumasi, and often said: *"I believe I shall see the goodness of the Lord in the land of the living"* (Psalm 27: 13).

I quoted some scriptures for strength such as *"I can do all things through Christ who strengthens me"* (Philippians 4:13) on the way to the toilet, and for me to be able to get up from the toilet seat. Without doing that I felt too weak to lift myself up.

I also used Psalm 74:16, 19, 20 a lot throughout my hospitalization and repeated especially: *"The day is Yours, the night also is Yours; You have prepared the light and the sun. Oh do not deliver the life of your turtledove to the wild beast! Do not forget the life of Your poor forever. Have respect to (remember) the covenant."*

Ms. Getsa Tsikata (a friend who is a Pharmacist and Associate of Joyful Way Inc. evangelistic singing group) gave my wife rides to the hospital in the mornings, and she often visited or called me to tell me to respond positively by faith to people who asked me about my health by telling them "I am the healed of the Lord." She was doing so to encourage the building of my faith for healing and deliverance.

CONFIRMATIONS OF ULTIMATE HEALING

I had a few meaningful dreams during my admission. A typical one I remember was an occasion when I found myself seriously preaching to a large group of people. When I woke up I knew that one day I would get healed and continue preaching.

During the recovery period, one of the most important words from the Lord impressed upon my heart was "seeking God", with reference especially to Colossians 3:1-3 where God enjoins us: *"If then you were raised with Christ, seek those things which are above, where Christ is, sitting at the right hand of God. Set your mind on things above, not on things on the earth."*

Since then, this has been a timeless major principle that I live by.

There were several revelations and spiritual insights given to loving and committed brethren who prayed, but I will recount only one or two. A group of women gathered every evening at 6pm in a home on the campus of the Kwame Nkrumah University of Science and Technology in Kumasi to engage in intensive prayers of intercession for me (many of them were wives of the campus professors, plus women of God I minister with or ministered to in the past when they were young, and some concerned women I did not even know etc.). Their leader (Dr. Patience Fleischer) later told me that during the initial stages of the prayer sessions they saw visions of coffins and signs of death, but as time went on they saw signs indicating life and healing for me.

A minister (who is a prayer warrior) and his prayer team came to pray for me one Sunday afternoon in Kumasi, and the minister mentioned that during the prayer he saw me healed and wearing my pajamas, walking around in the hospital.

During intercessory prayer for me by a family friend (Nana Abrah Adjei, an Elder in the Church of Pentecost) along with his wife Esther and their family in their home in Accra, one of the daughters (Gifty Adjei) saw me healed and sitting nicely in a chair.

CHAPTER THREE

TRANSFER TO KORLE-BU TEACHING HOSPITAL DIAGNOSIS OF THE ROOT PROBLEM, AND THE SOLUTION

THE STRANGE PHONE CALL TO MY FRIEND

The fluid that was oozing from the left side of my chest into a bottle continued day after day to a frustrating point where I wrote in my diary on 19th August 2009: "Liquid effusion is still not ceasing from my chest tube." That afternoon as I lay on my bed at Komfo Anokye Hospital, three and half weeks after admission, I thought of my good old classmate and close friend Dr. Samuel Somuah in Accra, and felt I should call him on my cell phone. I was not making or answering any phone calls during that period, and my wife was handling all the calls. I had been informed that Dr. Somuah was coming to visit me, but had not yet been able to do so. When he came on the line I simply told him I was thinking about him and decided to call him to say hi. During our conversation he was puzzled by my long hospitalization and the continual issuing of fluid from my chest. He expected that the fluid should have cease flowing after a few days. When I told him I had the condition for about three weeks, he responded that 21 days for such continuous copious fluid oozing from my chest was too much and too unusual, and a concrete solution had to be found. We had a short chat and ended there.

That mysterious phone call to Dr. Somuah on Monday August 17th 2009 was an important turning point in the entire scheme of affairs. Later he told me that after he hanged up the phone he could not shake off the thought and feeling of coming to visit me as soon as possible. He was about to leave for the USA, and decided to postpone his trip and come to Kumasi to visit me. He therefore came along with Miss. Augustina Haywood-Taylor (a banker and one of the Directors of our ministry — Fruitful Ministries International) on Wednesday 19th August 2011, the very day that I was quite down in my spirit. During our conversation he asked me: "Why don't you transfer to Korle-Bu Teaching Hospital in Accra (Capital of Ghana)?" I asked him why he thought I should do so, and his answer was that he believed there were more specialists with more medical equipment at Korle-Bu Hospital. Before then, when the only CT Scan machine at Komfo Anokye Hospital was not functioning, I had thought of going to Accra just for the scan and returning to Kumasi (if that was possible). My wife had also thought about possible transfer to Accra, because if we would finally leave for the USA, we would leave from Accra anyway.

DFFICULTY IN TRANSFER TO THE USA

Some people had questioned why I had not been flown to the USA (where I reside now) for medical treatment and was still waiting in Ghana without any appreciable improvement in my condition.

The problems involved in any travel were complex: First of all, none of the operating airlines at that time was willing to take me on board with the chest tube and accompanied continual fluid production, and even if they did, the tube and bottle plus oxygen and other equipment would have to come from the USA. Provision would have to be made on board to collapse three rows of seats for a screen to be put around the area to shield me from the other passengers, for me to pay for at least 50% of the total cost of all passenger seats sacrificed for me, and there should be a Doctor and a Nurse specially assigned to take care of me as well.

My daughter Hannah, on her own initiative, created a website that she thought she could use to raise funds for my support to the USA, and had contacted the Congressman in our Congressional District of the Hampton Roads. They put her in contact with the America Embassy in Accra, Ghana, for any arrangements for me to be transferred to the USA. She thereby contacted the American consulate in Accra, but it was still difficult for any definite plans to be made for my transfer to the USA. She tried to arrange for a Med-Plane which would be an ambulance aircraft sent exclusively for me, which would cost $100,000 that we did not have any US insurance to cover at that time. My Family Doctor in the USA had also cautioned my wife to be careful about any air travel because if the doctors in Ghana were not certain that my lungs were stabilized, they would collapse in mid-air at 35,000 feet.

PLANS FOR TRANSFER TO ACCRA

After agreeing with Dr. Somuah, he immediately started making some phone calls to initiate plans for my transfer to Accra. The next day we were told that the Directors of Komfo Anokye Hospital and Korle-Bu Hospital had consented to the transfer, and the physicians involved in my care in Kumasi had also agreed. Korle-Bu was alerted about my coming, and plans were made for us to leave on Thursday 20th August. However, Dr. Ken Abboa (the main person who initiated my treatment in Kumasi) wanted to come along with us, so the final arrangement was made for him to be able to go with us two days later.

I have to testify that Dr. Ken Abboa, Dr. Bedu-Addo, Dr. Betty Norman, Dr. Salamatu Attah Lawson, Dr. Madonna Lawson, Dr. Afua Pokuaa, Dr. Phillip Opare-Sem, Dr. Yaw Awuku, plus the Nurses of the Intensive care unit (Afrakoma, Matilda etc.) and their medical team in Kumasi did a good job by caring for me and helping to sustain me for a month before arranging for me to be transferred by an ambulance to Korle-Bu Teaching Hospital on Sat. 22nd August, 09. We sincerely thank them all.

Dr. Jonathan Lamptey (one of the young physicians at Komfo Anokye Hospital) was the doctor designated to take care of me in the ambulance from Kumasi to Accra along with a nurse Grazia Asiedu (incidentally an old daughter in the Lord whose mother also visited us in the hospital) accompanied by an assigned anesthesiologist. Dr. Ken Abboah (Chief Surgeon at Komfo Anokye) sat in front directing affairs with the driver. An anti-pain patch was stuck to my back, and was supposed to take care of every pain in my body for at least 12 hours.

About an hour after we left Kumasi on our way to Accra, the radio in the ambulance was tuned to the Christian Radio Station Spirit FM of Kumasi. My heart became stirred up with emotions which resulted in open cries and tears as I lay on my back, when a very melodic Christian song was played on the radio titled: *"He has not failed me yet."* The anesthesiologist who read into my sudden emotional expression spoke out to my wife and the Doctor plus the nurse to explain to them that my cries were not from any medical response or bodily pain, but resulted from how I had been moved by the song in the radio.

Considering all the pain I had gone through, I still believed that God loved me very much and was not unduly punishing me or being unkind to me. Deep down within me my heart ached for my sudden condition and its public magnitude, and somehow wondered when it was all going to be over.

ARRIVAL AT KORLE-BU TEACHING HOSPITAL IN ACCRA

We safely arrived at Korle-Bu Teaching Hospital in Accra at 2 pm on Saturday 22nd August 2009, earlier than expected, because the ambulance used its siren to obtain privileged passage along the highway and on streets in towns along the way, and especially in Accra where the traffic was heavy. I was taken in a wheelchair to the 4th floor of the Surgical Block. Dr. Samuel Somuah was around to give us a warm welcome, and was excited to see us. I remember him remarking with laughter: "Yes! This is Accra. We are going to take very good care of you."

I was expecting to remain there quietly for a while before most people heard about me, but I was wrong. To my surprise, at 4 pm (barely two hours later), visitors began to come in, and I wondered how the news went round so fast. By 5 pm my ward was almost full with a number of old friends, loved ones, and well-wishers. Family members heard about me and began to join more friends to visit during the days that followed.

MYSTERIES SURROUNDING THE PROBLEM

Up to that point the apparent incurable chest infection baffled everyone, and the doctors were literally at their wits end after trying all the best and most effective combinations of antibiotics available to them. The critical root problem was not diagnosed at Komfo Anokye Teaching Hospital in Kumasi. The doctors in Kumasi could not detect the major problem of the constant fluid filling my chest cavity, and thought it was only due to infection, until I came to Korle Bu Teaching Hospital in Accra.

One problem at the Komfo Anokye Teaching Hospital in Kumasi was that the only CT Scan machine that could have given a clearer indication of any damage to the tissues in my thoracic cavity, was out of order. I was told that the MRI machine was non functional as well. Only X-rays were taken and used for the diagnosis with ultra-modern equipment that gave very good images, but would not provide the definite clues to several detailed problems of organs and tissues.

Later on there was a general consensus that I might have had tuberculosis all along, that was latent and hidden without being discovered. I was therefore put on very potent TB medication that I had to take early at six in the morning. A TB test was therefore conducted on me by an expert, but the results were negative, but I was asked to continue taking my TB medication, "just in case". In fact, I rebelled against it one Friday morning, and refused to take the five huge brown tablets and a smaller tablet that had to be taken before the day started, the combination of which gave me terrible feelings in my body. As a result of my rebellion the doctors were not happy with me for that weekend.

It is interesting that when all the antibiotics had been tried with no visible or expected results to curb the infection in order to stop the flow of fluid from my chest, Dr. Abboah sat by my bedside one afternoon and commented to us: "Well, if you were to ask me for a final solution to this problem, my desire and suggestion as a surgeon will be to open up your chest, go in there, and do a total cleansing of the entire region and rid the place free of any infections and contamination". He emphasized how the Lord can miraculously provide healing along with the efforts of doctors. He then cited an example of a little boy who had massive cancer, but they managed to get into his abdominal cavity and get the region cleaned of all cancer cells. The boy who was very lean and dying has become healthy and vibrant today, and happily going to school.

I remember that before he left, he prayed with my wife and I, and one particular sentence in his prayer that stuck with me was: "Lord, grant him total healing, and even if you have to create new tissues in place of any damaged ones, Lord please do so".

In Kumasi, Henrietta and I, plus Pastor Peter, sometimes thought we saw the food I was eating going directly into the chest tube. There was one particular afternoon that I was lying in bed eating watermelon, and Peter was squatting by my bedside with a keen interest to particularly observe the contents of the chest tube, and he remarked: "Is that not the watermelon going into the tube? "

These observations were, however, dismissed by the doctors and nurses as far-fetched and funny because the only way for that to happen is to have contents of the esophagus leaking into the chest region. One physician later visited us, and we told him about the watermelon in the tube. He laughed at us and explained that there is absolutely no direct connection between the digestive and respiratory systems. He further explained that the color of the watermelon could mask the contents of some body fluids such as urine or any fluid exuding from the body, but the actual food particles would never be found in such fluid unless it passes directly into the chest cavity from the stomach or intestines.

The other argument was that if the esophageal contents were being released into the chest cavity, then no patient with a ruptured esophagus would look as healthy as I was physically (although I had pain, infection, and weakness). People with such problems would have severe fever, extreme pain, and become so sick within 24 hours that death symptoms would easily set in. Moreover I had been in the hospital for many days, and they could not imagine anyone with perforated esophagus surviving for so long and still eating normally, talking, laughing, and sleeping without extreme distress. Strangely enough, I was eating normally, and doing so three times a day! So, nobody paid attention to any consumed or digested food entering my chest region through any hole, and the primary focus was therefore placed on the chest infection.

FINAL DIAGNOSIS OF THE ROOT PROBLEM

When the CAT Scan of my chest cavity had not been made by the end of Monday evening (two days after arrival at Korle-Bu Hospital in Accra), I got a little upset and therefore pushed for it to be done, and was told to be patient because plans were being made for it to take place as soon as possible.

That evening, I felt strongly that something had not been discovered by the medical personnel all along. I mentioned it to my wife, and Mr. Ernest Commey, a close family friend and ministry partner who happened to be the only visitor around, so he and my wife came around my bed, and we prayed for the Lord to make the Doctors see and know

what the major cause of the infection and production of copious water from my chest really was.

In the morning of Tuesday 25th September 2009 at Korle-Bu Teaching Hospital in Accra (3 days after arrival from Kumasi) my wife Henrietta encouraged me to sit up and eat my breakfast instead of being fed in bed. I refused to heed her appeal, because when I sat down, the pains I felt were so intensive that I focused more on the pain instead of focusing on the food, and was always in a hurry to finish and lie down in the bed rather than enjoying the meal. She, however, succeeded in coaxing me to sit up.

The breakfast was porridge (farina) and bread with some eggs and butter, and while I began to eat, I looked at the chest tube on my left and strongly believed I saw the exact porridge going into the tube, so I called her to come and see.

Bro Ernest Commey was around, and observed it as well. My wife ran to call the doctors on duty to come and witness my observation. I challenged them to take a sample of the fluid in the tube to the lab and test the contents if it would not be the exact carbohydrate I was consuming. A syringe was therefore used to siphon what was coming immediately into the tube from my chest, in order to send it to the laboratory for analysis.

As Brother Commey was on his way to the lab with the sample, he met Dr. Joseph Glegg-Lamptey (the 2011 Head of Surgery Department at Korle-Bu Teaching Hospital, popularly known by us as Joe Nat of Joyful Way Singers), and he narrated the story to him. Dr. Joe Nat then commented: "I think I can now recognize what the real problem might be." Dr. Joe Nat then went to inform his surgeon colleagues of the Cardio-Thoracic Unit of Korle-Bu Teaching Hospital. Since I had a problem of collapsed lung and thoracic infection, doctors with chest and heart expertise were put in charge. A meeting was held on the issue and they agreed to conduct a simple test to verify the reality of food entering my chest cavity from my digestive system.

The Startling Discovery!

The team of surgeons of the Cardio-Thoracic Unit came to my ward at about 5pm on Tuesday 25th September 2011, and Dr Lawrence Sereboe (leader of the team) said to me: "Try to get up and sit down in the chair exactly as you sat in before. We are going to give you a simple test of sweetened methylene blue dye to drink, and observe what happens".

When I began to sip the solution, the blue liquid was immediately seen running from my chest into the tube within one second. With a stern face and mouth tucked in (as a dismal or grim sign), Dr. Sereboe turned round, gazed into my eyes, and immediately said: "Stop! You don't need to drink anymore. We need to open you up! Diagnosis of your basic problem is completed. There is no need for the CT Scan (scheduled for the next day). You have a ruptured (perforated) esophagus. We need to open you up immediately and fix the problem!"

It means that when I had the food poisoning at Tamale a month before, and vomited violently, I ruptured my esophagus (gullet) and that is why I felt the intense pain. In medical terms it is called **Esophageal Rupture** or **Boerhaarve Syndrome** which happens to the esophageal wall due to vomiting.

Dr. Mark Tettey (Dr. Sereboe's immediate assistant), with his head bowed down and intently gazing at the floor with a very tense face added: "And all the eating has to cease immediately!" My stomach sank and my heart jumped a beat, and I responded: "Whaaat?! You have to put me to sleep and open me up??"

You can't imagine the thoughts that raced through my mind along with the feeling in my heart, and the change in my facial expression, when my wife had just brought well-prepared dinner from the house that moment. On top of it, I have always dreaded being under general anesthesia in my life. My concern was that the doctors know how to put you to sleep using a chemical, but they have no opposite chemical to make you wake up by all means; and some people never woke up again after surgery!

Henrietta (being an experienced nurse) did her best to calm me down, and was rather more composed and pleased with the solution to the key problem than I was. I actually felt very much encouraged by her attitude and words.

Women, please take a cue from this, and watch how you react to your husbands or fiancees in the face of trials! She could have suddenly slumped into a sad and discouraged mode, and even started sobbing and uttering words of discouragement (or even blaming me for possibly contributing towards the tragedy), especially when she knew that the prognosis could be grim for a condition that should have been discovered and rectified several weeks before.

BOERHAARVE SYNDROME

About 56% of such ruptures are iatrogenic (i.e. due to medical instrumentation such as endoscopy). Esophageal perforation can also occur through accidental swallowing of bone and some other metal and sharp objects.

Rupture due to vomiting is a rare occurrence that accounts for 10% of such events. It was first described by Boerhaave in 1724 for a German patient who died from the problem before it was discovered during autopsy. The condition was therefore named after him. It is supposed to be the most deadly medical condition for the esophagus, and must be operated on within 24-48 hours. After 48 hours the victim has only 10% chance of survival; and that is even when the condition is diagnosed and operated on within that time frame.

An updated Medical Report by Praveen K Roy, MD, in December 2009 (Comments and Criticisms Editor, Cochrane Colorectal Cancer Group) stated as follows:

"Diagnosis of Boerhaave syndrome can be difficult because often no classic symptoms are present and delays in presentation for medical care are common. Approximately one third of all cases of Boerhaave syndrome are clinically atypical. Prompt recognition of this potentially lethal condition is vital to ensure appropriate treatment. Mediastinitis, sepsis, and shock frequently are seen late in the course of illness, which further confuses the diagnostic picture.

The mortality rate is high. A reported mortality estimate is approximately 35%, making it the most lethal perforation of the GI tract. Esophageal perforation is the most lethal perforation of the GI tract. Survival is contingent largely upon early recognition and appropriate surgical intervention. Mortality is usually due to subsequent infection, including mediastinitis, pneumonitis, pericarditis, or empyema. Patients who undergo surgical repair within 24 hours of injury have a 70-75% chance of survival. This falls to 35-50% if surgery is delayed longer than 24 hours and to approximately 10% if delayed longer than 48 hours. The best outcomes are associated with early diagnosis and definitive surgical management within 12 hours of rupture. If intervention is delayed longer than 24 hours, the mortality rate (even with surgical intervention) rises to higher than 50% and to nearly 90% after 48 hours. Left untreated, the mortality rate is close to 100%."

In the medical records of the entire world, the longest survived person without immediate surgery for Boehaarve syndrome was eight (8) days. Strangely enough, I existed with Boerhaave Syndrome for one month without knowing that I had the condition in Kumasi (during hospitalization for 4 weeks at the Intensive Care Unit of Komfo Anokye Teaching Hospital).

PREPARATION FOR SURGERY, AND THE OPERATION

I was then told that I would have to be transferred from the Surgical Block to the Cardio-Thoracic Unit (CTU) very soon for the procedure to start. They would carry out the operation at the CTU since it is tracheotomy involving my lungs and the entire thoracic region. I was expecting to be taken there later in the night or the next morning, but after about 30 minutes the transfer took place.

About 30 minutes after the discovery of the root problem, Dr. Sereboe came to my ward in the Surgical Block with some nurses in an emergency mode and firmly ordered: "You are being re-located with immediate effect to the Cardio-Thoracic Unit (CTU) of the hospital!" Nurses were ready with a stretcher to convey me to my new location.

My wife hurried to get our belongings together, and at 5:30 pm the nurses maneuvered and got me on a stretcher on wheels to my new ward. They informed my wife and Mr. Ernest Commey that 6 pints of blood would be needed for the surgical procedure. I was not even aware that behind me discussions were going on for blood donation among our friends. God had arranged for some of our Joyful Way Associates Christian brethren to be around for visitation, and Mr. Commey (also a Joyful Way Associate) consulted with them (Mr. Theophilus V. O. Lamptey and Mr. Kofi Ankama Asamoah) to arrange for blood donation for the surgery. They made such arrangements, in conjunction with Miss. Joana Abena Micah (an active member of Joyful Way) and rallied 6 volunteers of the group who came to the hospital early in the morning of the next day (day of the operation) to donate a pint of blood each. May the Lord richly bless all of them! I was completely oblivious to all these until the recovery period of that everything was narrated to me.

At the Cardio-Thoracic Unit, I was prepared for the surgery. Dr. Sereboe gave me a local anesthesia around my shoulder area, and created a central line with six outlets using my subclavian vein at my neck-shoulder region and explained that it was going to be the channel through which I would receive all of my medication, nutrients, and other intravenous fluids after the surgery until I was discharged. I remember him receiving a phone call as he busily made the incision etc., and telling the one: "I am busy now because we have an emergency, so I will call you back." At that time, I did not quite understand the extent of the seriousness and lethal nature of what had happened to me, and in my mind I wondered if the use of the word "emergency" was not overstated.

Before Dr. Sereboe left my ward he reiterated his initial caution to my wife and I, that if they went into my chest cavity and found the esophagus in a bad shape, they would remove it and follow it up with other procedures. My wife later told me that she was counseled in private about that possibility, and her answer to them was: "I do not mind what God would allow the final situation to be. All that I want is for him to be alive, and then we would figure out other issues."

I think that my ignorance played a significant role in helping me to be calm, and in part, my thoughts were also shaped by the fact that I had survived the ordeal for so long that its deadly nature would not have sank down well into my thinking even if I had been given real details of what was happening to me.

Above all *"God keeps in perfect peace the one whose mind is stayed on Him (trusts in Him) because he has put his trust in Him"* (Isaiah 26:3).

Another doctor later came into my room at about 8pm, and told me he had been assigned to prepare me for the surgery, which would take place the next morning. He informed me he would have to give me a close shave at specific parts of my body. I asked him why, and he gave me a simple explanation of the need to do so in order to eliminate electrical interferences that pubic hairs etc. could give to the electronic instruments. I was also told to remove my wedding ring and give to my wife for safe-keeping since that would also interfere with the electronics. It sounded to me as if I was being prepared for a final good bye of some kind! Wow!!

The Lord gave me calmness of mind and heart, and I was able to have a sound sleep in the night. I was later told that the seriousness of my condition prompted them to think of having the surgery right away in the night but they needed to prepare me and ensure that I had enough blood to stand by for transfusion.

My wife had gone home to lodge in the nearby home of our friends Dr. Samuel Somuah and his wife Dr. Mrs. Harriet Somuah (also a medical doctor). Harriet later told us that when she heard about the diagnosis, she searched for "Boerhaave Syndrome" on the Internet, and was frightened by the discovery of the dismal facts about the condition, but hid them from my wife because she did not want her to get scared.

The Day Of The Operation

I woke up in the morning of 26th August 2009 feeling a little strange about all that was happening and where I was heading in life. I wondered how my wife would be feeling deep within her, and thought about our children in the USA and our close friends who would not know what was going on. I read a short scripture and said some prayers as brief devotion. I managed to make a call to Mrs. Judith Agyemang in Kumasi to tell our Fruitful Ministries brethren and other friends to pray. The other call I made was to Dr. Ken Abboa at Komfo Anokye Teaching Hospital, who commented: "I believe things will go well because I trust Dr. Sereboe whom I worked with before in Kumasi, and is very good with his profession as well as Dr. Tettey, so rest your heart in the assurance that the operation will be successful." Dr. Abboah then prayed with me: "Dear Lord, we thank you for this new development. We pray that you will take total charge of the surgery for him to come out victoriously in Jesus' Name. Amen!"

My wife also made one or two phone calls to some of our friends to pray, and the information got to other loved ones from some of our Joyful Way and Fruitful Ministry brethren who launched into prayer for us. Someone for example told us that an announcement was made at the midweek prayer meeting at the main Calvary Baptist Church at Adabraka, Accra, for prayers to be offered for me because I was going into surgery.

My wife and I were clearly warned by the surgeons that they did not know what to expect, since the perforation had existed for too long, and it was expected that by then the perforated place in the gullet (esophagus) would be sore, infected, and possibly rotten.

34

They cautioned us that evening, and the next morning of the surgery, that they would have to remove my esophagus and feed me through a G-tube (Gastro tube) for 7 weeks, and then embark on another surgery to remove portions of my large intestines to reconstruct the esophagus. If that did not ultimately succeed, then I would not have any esophagus to live with, and I would have to be fed through a G-tube connected to my stomach for the rest of my life. Wow!

At about 8:00 am a team of nurses and two doctors came for me to send me upstairs. Just before we left the room, Dr. Sereboe gave me his phone to speak with Professor Rudolph Darko (Head of Surgery for Korle-Bu Hospital at the time) who was the on the line to tell me again: "Please know that just as we told you, we will have to remove your esophagus if we need to, and feed you through your stomach for a while and later try to reconstruct it using parts of your large intestines." I responded in agreement. Surprisingly, I was somehow concerned about my fate but was not very disturbed within me.

Soon after that I was wheeled out of my ward by a team of nurses and the two doctors to the Intensive care Unit of the Cardio-Thoracic Unit upstairs. On my way to the operating theatre and whiles they prepared me, I quoted scriptures by faith in my mind as I lay on the stretcher.

I remember that as they pushed me on a stretcher on the way to the operation theatre in the morning of Wed. 26th August, 2009, I thanked God, prayed for the Lord to be in full control, comforted myself with the thought that many people were praying for me in Ghana and around the world, took encouragement from the love plus prayers of my wife and family, and quoted scriptures as I lay on the stretcher. I encouraged myself and made every effort to hold on to my faith in the power of Jesus Christ and the Lord's grace through the prayers and scriptures, believing that God would not leave me in the middle of the road, but would take me through successfully. I told God that He should not let me die because it was not yet the time to leave. When I look back I realize that the entire episode from the beginning to that point was so shocking and so unexpected without any definite explanation that events had somehow bewildered me and made me a little numb. I had abandoned myself and my fate into God's hands to a large extent.

Some of the major scriptures that **I personalized and recited** to build much inner faith and comfort before and after the operation were:
"I have life in Jesus, and I have it abundantly" (St. John 10:10)
"I am healed by the stripes of Jesus" (1 Peter 2:24).
"If Jesus sets me free, I become free indeed" (St. John 8:36).

"In all these things I am more than a conqueror through Christ who loves me" (Rom. 8:37).

"Oh do not deliver the life of Your turtledove to the wild beast! Do not forget the life of Your poor forever. Have respect to (remember) the covenant" (Psalm 74:19, 20).

"I believe that I shall see the goodness of the Lord in the land of the living" (Psalm 27:14).

"We give thanks to the God and father of our Lord Jesus Christ" (Colossians 1:3).

"I overcome Satan by the blood of the Lamb and by the word of my testimony" (Rev. 12:11).

"I can do all things through Christ who strengthens me" (Philippians 4:13).

"Fear not, for I am with you. Be not dismayed for I am your God. I will strengthen you, yes I will help you, I will uphold you with My righteous right Hand" (Isaiah 41:10).

"I submit to God. I resist the devil and he will flee from me" (James 4:7).

"I humble myself under the mighty Hand of God, that He may exalt me in due time. I cast all my care upon Him, for He cares for me" (1 Peter 5: 6, 7).

One of my major prayers which I often pray to the Lord as a weapon against death threats by the devil is based on Colossians 3: 3, 4: *"I have died already, and my life is hidden with Christ in God. When Christ who is my life appears, I will also appear with Him in glory."*

I was initially taken to the Intensive Care Unit (ICU) of the CTU for final preparations. I even thought that was the place for the procedure, but realized it wasn't when one Doctor in green surgical outfit called to another: "Are you ready?" He replied "Yes". Then the two proceeded to push my stretcher through some open doors into the actual Operating Theatre. When I entered the large room with silver walls and two huge television monitors and other instruments around, then I knew I was really in business for life or for death. There were more people in the room than I expected, but it was later explained to me that several nurses and doctors performed different roles, and some medical students also come around to learn. Since my case was an interesting one, I suppose that it might have even attracted more personnel who came to learn important lessons.

I was taken off the stretcher and rolled on to the operating table itself. After one of the surgeons said: "let me give you some oxygen", an oxygen mask was placed over my nose and mouth (which I initially thought was a trick to put me to sleep without my knowledge), but the anesthesia was rather given to me as an injection. I remember feeling a little drowsy for a few minutes and then woke up to see that the operation was completed. One of the surgeons, Dr. Aniteye, later told me he was the anesthesiologist who collapsed my left lung where the problem was, and made me breathe through a respiratory machine, in order for them to clean around the lung.

GOD'S MIRACULOUS INTERVENTION

From my own observations, Dr. Lawrence Sereboe and Dr. Mark Tettey were the chief players, along with Dr. Gyang, Dr. Martin Tamatey, Dr.Aniteye, and Dr. Isaac Okyere. Dr. Entsua-Mensah and Dr. Ismail played some part as well. Other observers and contributors included Professor Rudolph Darko, Professor Frimpong Boateng, Dr. Joseph Clegg-Lamptey, and Dr. Kobina Nkyekyer. I have to admit that in my opinion doctors swear an oath of secrecy and confidentiality, and therefore I am only giving you information I fished out without complete knowledge of everything that occurred while I was sleeping under the surgical knife. I recall that on several occasions I wanted to get the very details of things, and Dr. Tettey would laugh and tell me: "Oh, the way you are asking your questions, then we should have had an actual video recording of the process to give to you."

The entire operation took about three and a half hours. I remember waking up and hearing someone saying: "We have finished!" I was gasping desperately for breath and made loud noises as I breathed, even with the big oxygen mask on. After a few minutes one of the surgeons remarked "I thing I will change that and give you the smaller nasal cannula (nasal tube) for oxygen because I think that is better for you." Later Dr. Aniteye told me he was the one that spoke and gave me the oxygen.

AT THE ICU AFTER THE OPERATION

I was wheeled to the ICU of the Cardio-Thoracic Unit where I was meticulously cared for and monitored for 2 days. Dr. Tettey came around a short while after I was sent there and I asked him: 'Was there a perforation in my esophagus as was suspected?' He opened his eyes and seriously replied: "Yes! And a big one too! Your chest cavity was very dirty, and we had to do considerable cleaning." Then I asked him further: "Were you able to fix it?" He replied: "Yes we did." You can't imagine the feeling of relief I had. Of course my mind was in a confused state (I believe), because if it was so bad, as they suspected, and they had not been able to rectify the problem, I should have seen my esophagus removed and a tube inserted into my stomach for nutrition. The truth is that the battle was not completely over, because there was the question still hanging in the air: "Will it finally work when the healing is completed?" We therefore had to continue intensifying the prayers.

The perforation, I was told, was about 3.5 cm wide at the lower portion of the esophagus where rupture by vomiting usually happens because that portion (just before the gullet enters the stomach) is not protected by the organs of the thoracic cavity.

Dr. Sereboe later told me that they had to use 10 vials of the most powerful antibiotic on the Ghanaian market at that time to clean the walls, and they even had to stop at some point because any further cleaning would destroy the walls. I was further given some daily doses of that antibiotic afterwards for a few days. One dose cost us 2.8 million (old) Ghanaian cedis a day! (The equivalent of $280 per one dose at the exchange rate in 2009).

Just to let you know that very good medical care cannot be afforded by the poor in our societies.

My wife came to the ICU about 15 minutes after the surgery, and I could see the relief (but also concern) on her face. She asked me how I was feeling, and she immediately lifted the blanket on me to look at my body; she did not speak, but I realized that she wanted to see the extent of the wound and to also see if indeed the worst had happened with the esophagus removed. I mentioned to her that they told me they had tried to fix the problem. She sat down by me, and a few minutes later Dr. Tettey came around and told her: "Please go home and sleep." She said good bye to me and left.

Electrodes were stuck to various parts of my body at the ICU to monitor my vital signs electronically. The next morning after the operation, before the nurses cleaned my body, I remember the nurse on duty monitoring my vital signs on a computer behind me and suddenly starting to sponge me with cold water for a while because my temperature had risen to about 3 degrees above normal.

GOD'S ABUNDANT GRACE

The power, grace, mercy, love of God was in full operation during the entire process. *The surgeons went in and found that the perforation in the esophagus was quite healthy physically when examined, which surprised everybody.* The report stated that the ends of the wounds bled freely, meaning the wound did not decay or become infected for one month! Thank you Jesus! Oh God, you are an awesome God!

The worst part of my situation was that I had been eating everything including the local foods that were even fermented before being prepared (e.g. the unfermented and fermented corn meals "banku", "agidi", "koko" and "kenkey"), plus bread, tea, cocoa drink, red hot pepper ("shito"), soup, fish, chicken, vegetables, fruits, plantain, cocoyam, yam, corn etc. and getting all the food and fluids plus medicine and water slipping into my chest through the hole in the esophagus to inundate and infect the entire chest cavity for one month! No wonder they initially found the bacterium *Klebsiella*, and later found *E. coli* bacteria, *Yeast*, and other microbes in the fluid samples.

Dr. Lawrence Serebour remarked after the surgery: "*Extraordinary things happen to extraordinary people*". I did not fully understand it at that time, but understood it more after I learned all the details.

In reality, several doctors find the complete repair of the damaged portion of the esophagus virtually impossible. I learn that they rather remove the torn portion, and do a bypass surgery to connect the stomach directly to the upper part of the esophagus after removing the perforated part (in which case the patient has to eat small meals at certain intervals).

When Dr. Tettey remarked to me that "We did what is not normally done and trusted that it would work", I later on understood what he meant. I learned that some portions of the thoracic epithelia (inside lining of the wall of my chest) had to be harvested and used to cover the hole and fortify the repair, after the initial stitching to close the gap. All these were done because they strongly desired to do the best for me to live normal life again. Praise the Lord!

IN THE RECOVERY WARD

Two days after the operation, I was sent to the recovery ward in the afternoon of Friday 28th August, sooner than most people expected. One doctor friend (Dr. Isaac Koranteng of Harvest Chapel in Accra) who visited me in the evening of my first day in the recovery ward (and paid several subsequent visits with his wife) was excited and commented to us: "We praise God for what he has done, because observers we telling me about the amazing things they saw when they opened you up at the operation theater. I was going to the ICU to see you but I was told you are now at the recovery ward. I said wow! That is really fast."

After the surgery extra care was taken to constantly balance my electrolyte levels every hour.

Daily injections of anti-coagulants were also given to prevent any blood clotting in my body (especially because I lay in bed for so long). I was fed intravenously for 2 weeks with liquid nutrients and fortified saline solutions (no solid or liquid entering my mouth), in order to ensure the complete healing of the repaired esophagus, along with an NG-tube (Naso-Gastric Tube) inserted through my nose into my stomach during the surgery to expel fluids, keep the damaged portion open, and aid the healing process. The N-G tube later became another great source of pain. After one week, the irritation of the tube in my throat began to give a sore throat that later hurt me so badly that I wanted it removed, but both Doctors Sereboe and Tettey insisted that it was very important for me to endure the pain and allow the tube to remain in my stomach through my throat to my nose where they sutured it for stability during the surgery.

At the ICU of Kumasi I had four or sometimes five other patients in the room with me, but in Accra I had my own suite at the Cardio-Thoracic Unit that had a bathroom, toilet, and kitchen. Several other wards at Korle-Bu Hospital had many beds and patients, anyway. I happened to be given a ward where I was alone. After my wife and the visitors left me to go home for the night I usually lay on my back and looked towards the ceiling, gazed into the air and towards the window in deep thought, wondering when I would get up totally healed and strong to live normal life. After consideration it was a better option for my wife to go home nearby and have a good sleep after toiling for me through the day. She knew she would not be able to sleep through the night if she remained by my side, and was concerned about falling sick in the midst of what we were dealing with, which would then make matters worse for us. At the ICU in Kumasi she would have had to sit through the night if she had decided to sleep there, and her seat was even inconvenient for her, and was partially improvised by us.

In Accra I tuned in to enjoy the Christian devotional songs from the FM stations coming through a small radio by my side that kept me company, as I prayed and meditated for some portions of the night. I pulled a cord attached to my bed to ring a bell to the Nurses station for help anytime I needed one, especially when I craved for some pain medication whenever the pain became unbearable.

Two weeks after the surgery I noticed that most of the skin in my soles and palms was peeling off. In fact, the entire skin in my palms and soles of my feet was ultimately peeled off and was replaced naturally by new skin. It was explained to me that this was caused by the multiple numbers of chemicals that had entered my body systems from the different drugs used for treatment.

Throughout my seven weeks of hospitalization, I lay a lot on my back because the chest tube did not permit me to lie down on my left, which also made it hard for me to turn to lie down on my right. This prolonged back sleeping position resulted in considerable pain around my pelvic (hip) area typically around my coccyx (the tiny tail bones at the very tip of my backbone) which persisted even several months after that.

As the days went by, Dr. Tetteh would come along to my ward and say: "We just need time and patience to wait for healing to take place." I could see that Dr. Sereboe could not wait to see the end results of the healing, which later delighted him when the initial testing showed no leakages. Dr. Tetteh remarked: "Everybody is very happy and glad."

In June 2011 when I visited Ghana two years after the surgery, I paid a delightful visit to Korle-Bu Hospital, to specially thank the doctors and nurses for all that they did for my wife and I. Everyone was indeed delighted to see me vibrant again. It was at the office of Dr. Tettey that he and Dr. Sereboe told me that they had dealt with several cases of perforated esophagus due to other causes, but my case was the first ever dealt with by the Cardio-Thoracic Unit at Korle-Bu Hospital that had resulted from violent vomiting. Dr. Tettey had just returned from Germany after presenting my case to the medical world at a seminar as the longest survivor of Beorhaave syndrome.

One young female physician from the Surgical Unit (Dr. Elizabeth Amanfu) who came to do routine procedures on me told me: "Everyone here in Korle-Bu Hospital says that looking at the kind of condition you brought here, you should not have been alive by now; and the conclusion of everyone is that you have not finished your work on earth. So, God kept you alive."

GOD'S GRACE AND RESCUE

"When the enemy comes in like a flood, the Spirit of the Lord will lift up a standard against him" (Isaiah 59: 19).

"Miracle man! Living miracle! As for you, you should have died four times! But you are still alive." That was a remark on phone by Rev. Dr. Theophilus Dankwa just before I was released from the hospital for initial recovery at home. He is a seasoned Christian who understood the miracle workings of God as former Senior Pastor, Accra Chapel, and the Travelling Secretary of the Ghana Inter-University Christian Fellowship for several years, who continued for many years as Travelling Secretary for the organization after it expanded to become Ghana Fellowship of Evangelical Students. He visited us at Korle-Bu Teaching Hospital with his wife Dr. Mrs. Virginia Dankwa (also a physician) and Rev. Osae-Addo (the current Pastor of Accra Chapel) plus some of the congregation members. They actively prayed for us and assisted us in other loving ways, and knew the details of what had happened to me.

The statement of Rev. Dankwa might have sounded like a joke or an exaggeration, but I thought to myself that probably he might not know that he was right in the way he put it. Why? Because I noted four instances when I could have easily died, which were as follows:

1) The rupturing of my esophagus paved the way for fatality before I left Tamale for Kumasi 48 hours after the problem started. I had only 10% chance of survival at that point, and anything tragic could have happened on the way in the vehicle for the 7-hour drive to Kumasi, when I did not know that there was great danger residing in my body cavity.

2) If Dr. Ken Abboa and his wife had not insisted on taking me to the emergency room of Komfo Anokye Teaching Hospital in Kumasi around 10pm in the night of Sunday 26th July, 2009 after arrival from Tamale, I would have definitely passed away in my sleep when I was unaware that fluid had filled my chest cavity and collapsed my left lung, and was about to collapse my right lung as well.

3) I was so weak during the time of the surgery, and my body had gone through so much struggle that the body could have given up for me to

remain permanently asleep when the anesthesia was employed to put me to sleep. My body was very exhausted. My electrolyte balance was considerably low especially during the latter stages of my hospitalization from the loss of so much fluid and accompanied essential ions from my body, which could have led to serious malfunction of my nerves, brain, spinal cord, heart, and blood vessels in particular. The massive infection from several microorganisms had given serious systemic infection that created severe septicemia (high toxicity in my blood stream) which could have shut down several organ functions within my body and precipitate my death.

4) The initial food poisoning so powerfully shook my body with chills, dizziness, stomach churning, and vomiting that obviously resulted in some intestinal contents wrongly entering into my respiratory system (aspiration) in addition to leaking of food through the perforation in my esophagus, and gave me excruciating pain in my chest region, plus toxicity that gave me very sickly feeling, all of which pointed to fatality. We received reports about people who died of food poisoning in the past and even while I was still in the hospital. The Lord assisted the medical team in Tamale to combat the toxins, sustain my body with different Intra Venous infusions all night, and took diligent steps to keep me alive. I convulsed in terrible pain through that night in the hospital bed at Tamale, with respiratory obstructions and breathing problems, but the Lord kept me alive by His infinite grace.

OTHER COMMENTS ABOUT GOD'S DELIVERANCE
I heard (and keep hearing) from those who really saw, knew, and understood (or understand after hearing what happened) that it is sheer miracle and God's Grace that I am alive. One year after the incident, the wife of one of the surgeons involved in diagnosing and supporting my treatment remarked to me on phone; "My husband tells me that looking at the condition which you brought to the hospital, there is no reason why you are still alive (humanly speaking) if it were not by the grace of God."

In the night of October 2, 2010 I happened to be on Facebook doing some counseling when one medical doctor popped up for a chat with the words: "Hi Dr., the miraculous survivor of Boerhaave Syndrome." He later stated to me that he was among the surgeons that operated on me on 26th August 2009 at the CTU of Korle-Bu Hospital.

A physician at Komfo Anokye Hospital in Kumasi who did not know me, and had no idea that I was lying close by, came to my ward one day in August 2011 with Mrs. Vic Abboah (wife of the Head of Surgery at Komfo Anokye Hospital at the time) on a visit and commented when she saw the initial X-ray of my chest at the nursing station: "The person with this X-ray should not be alive by now!" Then Vic quickly told her: "That person is still alive, and is lying over there!" The physician then turned and gazed at me with a bewildered face.

GOD HAS DONE IT AGAIN!

On the Sunday morning of 6th September, 2009, Dr Sereboe passed by my ward to see how I was faring, on his way to church, and you could see how expectant he was to find out if healing had taken place. He mentioned the he was being tempted to remove the N-G tube so quickly because the body produces copious amounts of saliva, and if the esophagus were still leaking, then a large amount of saliva should have been leaking through the chest tube into the collecting bottle outside.

After the church service he came around, and made me drink methylene blue dye (same as was used to diagnose the problem) to see if any drops could be found in the chest tube. The test was negative. Praise God! The healing process has indeed worked! OUR FAITHFUL GOD HAD DONE IT AGAIN! The ruptured esophagus has been repaired! The Naso-Gastric tube was removed, which was quite a painful process for me as the tube was pulled all the way from my stomach, out through my nostril. I actually did some screaming due to the intense discomfort as the tube came out.

He then advised my wife to start me with some liquid diet for me to start eating again after two weeks of intravenous feeding. She went home nearby and prepared me some custard and tea that I enjoyed after a long time when nothing had entered my mouth.

On Wednesday 9th September, 2009, exactly two weeks after the surgery, the chest tube that had been inserted into my body for seven weeks, was finally removed. No longer any fluid coming from my chest! You cannot imagine the joy and relief, and excitement! Thank you Jesus! Praise the Holy Name of Jehovah!

One morning, after the N-G tube had been removed and I was now able to drink liquids, I managed to walk to the weighing scale a few meters away in the corridor, and with the assistance of a nurse, weighed myself. I was stunned to discover that I had lost 50 pounds!

On the 14th of September 2009, Gastrophosate (better alternative for Barium because it is not chalky and not nasty to swallow) was used for the familiar machine "Barium Swallow Test" to see if my esophagus had any leakages, and it was found to be negative! The gratitude, joy, and praises of my wife and I could not be measured! I remember returning to the ward, and lying in bed with my hands raised in prayers of thanksgiving, and my wife quickly taking me pictures in that mode.

I spent a few more days at the hospital because one or two mosquitoes managed to sneak in to bite me and give me slight malaria that raised my body temperature, which had to be dealt with before they could let me go home.

READY TO GO HOME!

After the surgery, I spent two and half weeks at Korle-Bu Teaching Hospital for the initial recovery process to be monitored. People were encouraged by my fast recovery and some were even surprised including some concerned doctor friends who followed my progress, and were praying for me, visited or called to wish me well on phone.

On the day when we had signed the papers and paid our bills for us to officially leave the hospital, my wife was in high spirits for us to leave, while my attitude was surprisingly opposite of hers. I had slept for so long in the hospital bed that I seemed to have forgotten that there was another bed waiting for me at home. My body was somehow stuck to my bed, and I had gotten used to my "new home" in the hospital. I would not easily get out of the bed and dress up for us to go home! The good ward of the CTU that appeared like a small rented apartment made me feel so much at home. On top of it, my air condition that was broken down for a long time but had been fixed that afternoon, made me feel like enjoying the room a little more.

May be the experts in psychology and medical idiosyncrasies could give me a better explanation. I had not even taken into consideration that occupancy of the room is paid for each day, and other patients would be waiting to be admitted into the ward. We would finally leave, but as my wife kept waiting and asking me to get out of the bed for her to dress me up, I kept telling her to kindly let me sleep just for a little while. Finally I heard her praying and rebuking the devil who would not let us go home, and for God to grant me the grace to get up for us to get ready and leave.

I took that prayer of my wife lightly at that moment, but looking back now, I think she was right. A hospital bed is not a place to enjoy sleeping after you have began to recover and have the chance to go home for further recuperation. The enemy and the flesh conspired to play tricks on my mind, to get me bound to the hospital even when God had opened the door for me to be free.

Finally I was discharged in the afternoon of Wednesday 16th September 2009, and I wrote in my diary: "Finally discharged from Korle-Bu Hospital Cardio-Thoracic Center! Praise God! Thank you Jesus!"

THANKS TO THE ALMIGHTY GOD FOR HIS GRACE AND MERCY, AND THE PRAYERS OF MY FAMILY AND THE SAINTS (INCLUDING YOURS) THAT KEPT ME ALIVE!

SPECIAL THANKS TO ALL THE DOCTORS, NURSES, AND FRIENDS FOR THEIR EFFORTS, CONTRIBUTIONS, AND SACRIFICES TO KEEP ME ALIVE.

CHAPTER FOUR

THE IMPORTANCE OF HOSPITAL WORK AND HOSPITAL VISITATION

The 28th of August 2009 was our 27th wedding anniversary, which was two days after the operation was performed on me. It was interesting celebrating our anniversary on a hospital bed under the conditions of intense pain, but God was and is still the God of our lives, and we prayed to thank Him for His wisdom, grace, and mercy.

While I was in Ghana it also occurred to me that 2009 was my 40th year of ministry which deserved celebration, and I was considering discussing it with my wife for us to have at least a simple time of praises and thanks to God for His goodness and mercy in choosing many of us to manifest His power, grace, and glory through us. It is interesting that I ended celebrating it in pain, perplexity, and in hospital, by experiencing more of God's goodness and mercy, and the love of friends and family.

I had never been hospitalized before, but I happened to receive a full dose (if not more than my fair share) of hospital life for seven good weeks, and in a unique way that took me through the experiences in the two largest hospitals in Ghana (and therefore hospitals in a typical developing nation) consecutively. I also had a unique experience of being carried in an ambulance between the two largest cites of Ghana for 170 miles, rather than the short trips that most people have from their homes to the hospital in an ambulance.

THE LABOR OF HOSPITAL PERSONNEL

When I was young, my number one dream was to become a surgeon in the army. I loved the military force and the medical career, and wanted to have a good combination of both. God, however, allowed circumstances to be created that indirectly "foiled" my personal plans, for me to still major in the biological sciences that have several medical implications, and be a college professor instead. This I realized, was in accordance with my natural talents and spiritual gifts that God had planned to make full use of in training people for career development and ministry, and to enable me become a greater agent of blessings for the church of Jesus Christ and society, rather than being limited to the hospital.

In the hospital I had the unique opportunity to clearly see real hospital life, interact with doctors plus nurses and hospital workers, and gain considerable understanding of what really goes on now in our local hospitals. In reality, we must deeply appreciate the work done for all of us by hospital personnel. The labor in our hospitals is intensive and tough. It is not often attractive due to many unpleasant and even depressing and devastating or tragic conditions one has to deal with (accidents, blood, wounds, trauma, very repulsive odors, disturbing deformities, incapacitation, gradual or sudden deaths, hostile and uncooperative or even dangerous patients, exposure to toxins and dangerous radiation, harmful microorganisms, instruments with potential to harm you if something goes wrong etc.).

There is so much to narrate, but I wish to be brief and try to stay on course in accordance with the primary theme of this book — to let you know how frail we are as humans, the wickedness of the enemy of our souls, God's wisdom and love plus His awesome ways of working, and rescue plans that God puts into operation for His beloved children.

In summary, I saw the differences between diligent, loving, caring, efficient, professional, and good nurses (and even doctors), as compared with hospital personnel who are either bored, incompetent, disenchanted, lazy, careless, carefree, prejudiced, callous, and uncaring. I noticed the difference between those who work because they love the profession, and others who work as mere duty for a living.

Many of the nurses did a great job, and were very friendly and very loving. Most of the nurses patiently drew blood and gently gave me injections, but in isolated cases a few nurses had less patience, and hurriedly or quite callously injected needles and hurriedly took vital signs (temperature, blood pressure, pulse, and respiratory data). They were either in a hurry to finish what they were doing and continue with their preferred agenda, or had some roughness as habit (as I discerned). I noticed that some medical personnel have done the different procedures so often that the particular states of individual patients were not being taken into consideration. In a few instances when I complained, it sounded as if I was rather too sensitive and "not being a brave man" to endure the pains.

We wish to make a quick mention of Matilda and Afrakoma, the two Nursing Sisters who supervised other nurses and activities at the intensive care Unit at Komfo Anokye Hospital. These two senior nurses were very friendly and gentle, and did a great job along with the doctors. At Korle-Bu

Teaching Hospital both day and night nurses were great (Margaret Yeboah, Joyce Atiemo, Mercy Ashley, Comfort Bawa, Letitia Owusu, Bridget Yitamkey, Portia Mills, Oparebea, Ellen Amoakohene, Comfort Mensah, Jane Khasem etc.).

Miss. Rita Appiah and her physiotherapy team did a good job on me, although I sometimes gave them a hard time by refusing to cooperate and do the chest and other body exercises they led me to do.

Influence Of Present World Situation At The Workplace

It appeared to me that the present world tension, economic hardships, lack of basic resources and equipment, low salaries, overwhelming personal problems and challenges, all come together in a formidable mixture to lower morale, enthusiasm, professionalism, efficiency, and productivity in all sectors of our workplace, including our hospitals and medical facilities.

Ensuring that they finally get the right medication for patients, can be sometimes trying for medical personnel, in addition to everything else they have to deal with. It is very interesting that on several occasions when prescriptions were written for us to purchase drugs, the hospital personnel directed us to specific pharmacy stores where they were doubly sure that the right medicine would be given to us. This is because many quack and fake pharmacy stores have sprang up, that are operated by charlatans and deceitful money-makers who sell cheap powerless medications with no therapeutic properties. This, we are told (even from testimonies of the public), has caused the death of people from ordinary sicknesses and common illnesses that could have been easily cured if only the correct medication was administered at the onset.

IMPORTANCE OF HOSPITAL VISITATION

I learned the importance of hospital visitation and ministering to the sick in their distressed conditions. For example, a doctor friend (Dr. Letitia) from another clinic came around and saw that we needed to make my hospital ward more lively, so she came back the next day with a beautiful vase of flowers to decorate my table, saying that "the place looked dry" when she first visited us. That is how thoughtful good friends are.

Visitation by family members, friends, and other loved ones plus even strangers with good hearts, collectively constituted a balm that promoted my comfort, hope, strength, and health in the hospital.

I appreciated every single visit, and sincerely thank everyone who visited me, and phoned my wife and I in the hospital, and also visited us at home during my time of recovery. I was highly impressed by some devoted Christians and Ministers of the Gospel who have made it their primary aim to visit the sick and suffering in hospitals early in the morning and during the evening hours to pray for them, and offer them some love and comfort by their presence and words of hope. Some of them went further to call me from time to time to check on me and establish friendship.

I learned about the different attitudes, facial expressions, behavior, and actions of many visitors and well-wishers who came to see me. The genuine look of compassion and deep concern to see me getting out of bed and be strong again was very obvious in the faces and actions of many Pastors, family members, ministry leaders, friends and people I had never met before, or who knew me without my knowledge of them. I noticed that the majority of people visited out of love and compassion. Some people's visit was very short, but their loving or spiritual and compassionate presence left lasting impressions with me.

I remember Dr. Bedu Addo (leader of the medical team that attended to me at Komfo Anokye Teaching Hospital) commenting a few days after I was admitted: "As for you I expect that this room should be very full of people." He implied that I was well-known across Ghana, and many would be touched to come over to visit and wish me well. Indeed I received many visitors across a wide spectrum in Kumasi, and in Accra. Some travelled from far places. As the news spread around, more people would have streamed to the hospital in Kumasi, but some heard that I had been transferred to Accra, and some people came round to look for me after I had left.

A number of people came to visit when I was asleep and did not want to disturb me, so they left quietly (for example, Rev. Ransford Obeng, senior pastor of Calvary Charismatic Church in Kumasi who came around one night). I was later told about their visit, or do not even know that some people came around when I was asleep. The hospital security and the nurses on duty were quite strict to maintain my peace and comfort, and regulated the number of visitors considerably, especially after regular visiting hours.

There was one Sunday afternoon after the surgery in Accra when my room was filled with about 15 visitors, and the security lady on duty aggressively drove everyone out because the visitation period was over, and in addition, the medical team was about to come for routine examination. I know that some visitors were upset with her, especially because they had travelled from afar.

One pathetic case was that of a beloved mother in Accra who was seriously interceding for me, and out of compassion, boarded an airplane from Accra (Ghana's Capital) to Kumasi to see me in the hospital, but got there at a crucial time when the doctors were performing some procedures on me (according to the nurses), and was therefore not allowed to see me. She later visited me at home with her daughter while I was recovering and told us.

I learned of another classic example of love and compassion when one of our Fruitful Ministries active members (wife of a pastor) narrated to me that when she came with her husband to visit me in Kumasi, she was not expecting to see me in the terrifying state she found me with fluid oozing from my chest through a tube, and so debilitated by the illness, and thought she would finally lose me (as she put it). She was three months pregnant, and the sudden intense chill she had in her stomach, and the shock that followed, made her start to bleed as soon as she left me and was descending the stairs in the hospital. That resulted in a miscarriage.

THE BEST WAY TO HANDLE THE SICK AND AFFLICTED

I learned the art of proper and best ways and modes to handle the sick and suffering. Some of them were:

1) The words we speak

Words are very important and very powerful in such circumstances, and should be carefully chosen and fitly spoken for the best results. I had an abundance of such edifying and comforting words that promoted healing of mind and heart.

A number of people, however, exercised the notion (and a principle) that the sick need a very quiet environment to be calm and to create an atmosphere that would speed up their recovery, and they should not therefore speak unless they had to, and should not be engaged in any form of conversation. Such people therefore said very little, and even tried to silence me whenever I tried to speak to them.

2) The gifts we bring

Several people brought encouraging and essential items, typically cards, flowers, fruits, juices, bottled water, and other food items. Some people visited and parted with some monetary gifts to help with expenses. Before visiting, some loved ones even called to ask what they should bring along.

3) The Prayers We Offer

I took particular notice of the varieties of prayers of different people who visited me, or prayers offered on phone. Some were very empathetic (put themselves in my shoes); some were out of shock; others out of sadness and sorrow, while some were straight ministry out of their normal selves as usual. From experience I learned also that people will usually sense the spirit behind my words, attitude, deeds, and I should therefore be aware and be as sincere as possible, and always perform to the best of my ability.

In my distressed state, my reactions towards different prayers were complex and mixed. It will interest you to know that some people could not simplify their prayers which sometimes "got on my nerves" or distressed rather than edifying me; the same thing applied to some of the exhortations and speeches. It was later explained to me that my mixed and sometimes negative emotions were the normal symptoms of someone who is severely sick and suffering. I learned important lessons of how to carefully and wisely offer the most appropriate comfort and encouragement to the sick and suffering.

I recognized that sometimes the patient or an attendant must properly explain the patient's condition to a visitor to facilitate the best interactions. I remember a good friend who often visited and prayed with me in Kumasi. He even followed up to visit me in Accra after I had been transferred there from Kumasi. One morning he visited me at Komfo Anokye Hospital and started his parting prayers as usual with some singing. He saw that I was quiet as he sang (unlike me) so he stopped and asked me to sing along with him. He did not really know or understand the state of my previously collapsed lung and the subsequent respiratory and speech difficulties, so I told him I could not sing. My collapsed lung was not fully expanded yet to allow the ability to sing. He understood and humbly continued singing alone, and then prayed for me.

BETTER UNDERSTANDING OF THE SICK AND SUFFERING

I have now gained a better understand of the different moods and emotional upheavals that sick people experience, and I am more sympathetic with the condition and behavior of anyone who falls ill.

It was strange to me that I hated the ringing of my cell phone, though I was not the one handling it, and the sound of the phone often gave me a sickly and obnoxious feeling. Being a great lover of melodic music, the devotional songs of FM radio stations at night that came from a little radio brought by one of the nurses on night duty, was a huge balm for my soul and spirit especially around 2am to 4am when I stayed awake at Komfo Anokye Hospital after a few hours of sleep.

PERMANENT IMPACT OF THE WORDS AND PRAYERS OF FRIENDS

Some words of encouragement, scriptures, and prayers of beloved ones stuck deeply in my mind, and energized my spirit from time to time. For example a beloved Christian friend Vincent Akwaa (a counselor at Charismatic Christian Church in Kumasi) and his wife Christina (whom I knew as Christina Mimi Hagan when she was a student in Wesley Girls High School in Cape Coast, Ghana in the late 1970's) visited me one Sunday evening at Komfo Anokye Hospital. The wife drew my attention to a particular scripture, and quoted it to me before her husband prayed, and Christina emphasized to me that I should draw confidence from that word in the Bible, and regard it also as a promise of the Lord. She did not know that it is one of the scriptures I have taken note of in the Bible in the past.

That scripture says: *"The day is Yours, the night also is yours; You have prepared the light and the sun. **Oh, do not deliver the life of your turtledove to the wild beast!** Do not forget the life of Your poor forever. **Have respect for the covenant**"* (Psalm 74: 16, 19, 20).

50

Since then I have used this scripture in prayer with my wife countless times, especially the words: *"Oh, do not deliver the life of your turtledove to the wild beast! Have respect for (remember) the covenant"*.

As I ponder over that scripture, my mind is drawn to my Blood Covenant with Jesus who has saved me, plus all that God has deposited in my life to use for His Kingdom, and my relationship with the Master.

In the afternoon of Sunday 6th September 2009, our friend Commodore Geoffrey Biekro (Chief of Staff of the Ghana Armed Forces) and his wife Letitia came to visit us after church service at Royal House Chapel in Accra where they are members. Before they left Commodore Biekro came very close to me and prayed for me. A statement from his prayers that stuck in my mind was: "Lord, as you said in Daniel chapter 11 verse 32, that the people who know their God shall be strong and make exploits; Lord, make Him strong for him to come out and continue to make exploits for Your Kingdom."

During a hospital visitation one Sunday afternoon, I remember that Professor Stephen Addai, former Director of Ghana Institute of Management and Public Administration (GIMPA, Accra) jokingly (but seriously) told me on arrival in the ward at Korle-Bu Hospital (with a warning finger): "Look, we leave (i.e. die) according to age, so be careful!" In other words, those of us who are apparently younger than some of them should not die and leave them (the older generation) behind to fight the remaining battles. That was a timely warning and encouragement for me to prop up my faith and hope to fight through the storm and stay alive.

CHAPTER FIVE

THE IMPORTANCE OF PRAYING FOR ONE ANOTHER

*"Confess your trespasses (sins) to one another, and **pray for one another, that you may be healed**. The effective fervent prayer of a righteous man avails much (has great power in its effects)"* (James 5: 16)

My wife Henrietta narrated to me that one morning at about 3am, in the heat of affairs in Kumasi, she was tossing and turning in bed, and had been unable to sleep or even pray with a focused mind during the night because of my situation that was not getting any better. In the midst of all the inner pain and confusion a lady called her unexpectedly and said she felt led to pray with her. She did not mention her name, and just as she was going to ask for her name at the end of the prayer, she hurriedly hung up the phone. Up till now she does not know who that person was, but after that prayer, she felt very relieved and could sleep soundly for at least an hour before getting ready to come to me at the hospital at 6 am.

This underscores the necessity of allowing the compassion of God to flood our hearts, for the Lord to stir our hearts to pray and intercede for one another just when prayer is needed.

So many ministers, men and women of God, and friends, prayed over me directly in hospital and at home or over the phone, that it is impossible to mention all the names. We wish to express our deep and sincere thanks to all of them.

POWER OF CORPORATE PRAYERS

One of the most important factors my wife keeps emphasizing is the need for extensive prayers of intercession, regarding the ordeal we went through and for similar incidents that we hear about in the lives of other people. As I wrote this manuscript she kept reminding me to stress on the importance of praying fervently for one another. She always says and believes that a lot of collective intercessory prayers of many people around the world ascended to God's Throne in Heaven to save my life.

Indeed we have come to clearly understand the importance of corporate and fervent intercession in times of emergency and trials. As much as all of us try to keep our personal and family secrets secret, or keep to ourselves what we consider very personal, we have seen and understood the importance of making known your important needs, and allowing people to bear you up in prayer.

Some needs demand corporate prayer, corporate anointing, corporate intervention, and corporate support. The way the enemy came in swiftly to take me out in the twinkle of an eye, in order to devastate my family, create grief for loved ones, and throw Christendom into sorrow and confusion for people to ask: "Where is thy God?", was not something to play any 'macho' games with, or assume any air of super-spirituality, shyness, and secrecy and try to fight such a gigantic battle alone.

I have come to believe that some catastrophes, family tragedies (including violence, separations, divorces, perversions, ruining of children, financial or property losses etc), church and ministerial devastations (backslidden brethren, bitter quarrels, church break-ups, immoral explosions, demise of evangelistic organizations, emergence of false prophets and deceptive men and women of God who cause havoc in the Body of Christ etc.), destructive habits plus problems in personal lives, fatal or disabling diseases, as well as even some deaths and tragic accidents of people, *could have been prevented IF SPIRITUALLY-MINDED, LOVING, AND CONCERNED PEOPLE WERE MADE TO BE AWARE, AND WERE STIMULATED TO SINCERELY CRY TO GOD IN FAITH-DRIVEN SPIRITUAL INTERCESSION.*

Few Examples Of Prayers For Me

As soon as Dr. Ken Abboa discovered the problem at Komfo Anokye Teaching Hospital in Kumasi, he told me the next day at the ICU that he had informed a Doctor friend who is a prayer warrior and runs a prayer group in Cape Coast (Ghana) to start praying with his intercessors for me.

The information quickly traveled outside Ghana, and a professor, for example, visited me in the hospital in Kumasi and told me that he learned of it within the first few days through a phone call from another Ghanaian professor who was on holidays in London, England, asking him to pray for me. He was quite surprised that someone in London was telling him about it in the very city where I was hospitalized, while had had no wind of the incident. A pastor in Accra also told me during his visit at Korle-Bu Hospital that a friend in London had mentioned my condition to him on phone that day.

The leaders of our ministry (Fruitful Ministries international Inc.) in Accra and Kumasi in particular, as well as other branches in various cities of different Regions in Ghana (Techiman, Sunyani, Tamale, Obuasi, Nkawkaw, Agogo, Dunkwa, Konongo, Koforidua, Tema, Elmina, Cape Coast, and Takoradi), organized a lot of prayers, and engaged in constant serious prayers for us.

One interesting story that set all of us bursting into laughter was an account by one beloved Fruitful Ministries sister and her friends who visited us at home in Accra during the recovery period. She told us: "I woke up in the morning of 26th August, 2009 with a fever, and was feeling terrible as I cared for my little baby. Then I received an early phone call asking me to pray because Dr. Kisseadoo was about to go into surgery. Then all of my fever vanished! I called another Christian brother who is a prayer warrior and told him to pray, and I frantically asked him for advice. He suggested that I should gather some people around for a serious group prayer for at least one hour before the surgery begins, so I called two of my friends to come around, and we prayed fervently for you." The dramatic way in which she described how her fever vanished, is what prompted the laughter.

Some people were mysteriously prompted by the Lord to pray, and that makes us sense the dimensions of the spiritual attack that was in operation, and the Lord's plan to defeat the enemy on our behalf. For example, one morning in August 2009, Mrs. Comfort Gyermeh, the wife of Rev. Dr. Stephen Gyermeh (Senior Pastor, Church of the Living God, Hyattsville, Maryland) was sweeping in her kitchen when I came heavily on her mind and heart. She had not seen me for more than a year. She could not shake me off her heart and mind, so she stopped sweeping and threw the broom down. She then went to her phone to call a Christian sister whom she knew would be in constant touch with me, just to find out where I was at that moment in time (she knew I would normally be in Ghana in July/August of every year for ministry and some research). The sister confirmed that indeed I had gone to Ghana on my usual mission trip, and some kind of tragedy had struck. She immediately launched into intercessory prayer all by herself, and she told me she could not continue her sweeping until her heart was content with the level of prayer she had offered. Her husband and other congregation members of their church later engaged in prayers for me as well, and one church member told me that they depended on God's promises to protect His ministers at the battlefield of ministry in Mark 16: 17-18, for their prayers.

There are testimonies of many people who sincerely interceded and lamented on my behalf worldwide, especially in Ghana, but we had no knowledge that news about me had travelled that far. Catherine Hagan, a beloved daughter in the Lord who made time to visit me in the hospital in

Kumasi, later told me that she constantly told God in prayer to touch and heal me because she could not afford to lose me.

Mrs. Dora Ohene Frempong (wife of Rev. Roger Ohene Frempong, Senior Pastor of the Sunyani Branch of Calvary Charismatic Church) was rejoicing on phone for the victory when I called after arrival in the USA, and said: "Hmm, we have prayed and wept a lot as we cried to God around here in Sunyani (Brong-Ahafo Region of Ghana)". Before my transfer to Accra, they were organizing to visit me as a group, led by Rev. James Appiah Kubi who was the President of the Sunyani Gospel Ministers Network, and who is our ministry representative in Sunyani, helping to organize our Family Life Seminars and Annual Pastors and Leaders Seminars.

Doctors and nurses in the hospitals of Kumasi and Accra came to us reporting of phone calls and messages they received in the hospitals from several places in Ghana to look out for me at Komfo Anokye and Korle-Bu Hospitals.

A pastor in Kumasi, who is a prayer warrior with experience in deliverance, launched into prayer with his congregation for me, and came to me at Komfo Anokye Hospital to emphasize to me: "My brother, if many serious prayers had not been offered on your behalf, you will not be among the living by now". The second time he visited, he mentioned to me that as he was praying for me at home the day before, he felt a strong attack on him during the prayer, indicating that a very high level of spiritual attack was in progress.

A beloved Christian brother, who is a lecturer at Kwame Nkrumah University of Science and Technology (KNUST) in Kumasi, came to the hospital to prophetically expose and confirm one particular unexpected source and level of attack in progress. The high level of attack was confirmed by many men and women of God in and outside Ghana, with warnings to take special precautions.

Lecturers and members of the Staff Christian Fellowship of KNUST in Kumasi swung into aggressive prayer when they learned about what was happening. I was told that at an initial meeting for prayer at KNUST, the leader emphatically declared to all the lectures and their wives who had assembled: "We are NOT going to allow this sickness to result in death!" I had met the Staff Fellowship for a talk and great fellowship on KNUST campus just before traveling from Kumasi to Tamale where the tragedy occurred.

Several members of the Kumasi Ministers Fellowship, who participated in our Annual Pastors and Church Leaders Seminar two weeks before, began fervent prayers, led by Pastor Nicholas Awuah Sarpong (of Maranatha Evangelistic Ministries), who is the secretary of the Kumasi Ministers

Fellowship and is also our Fruitful Ministries Resource Person and the Coordinator for our Annual Pastors and Church Leaders Seminar.

Pastor Peter Shiltoncole of Empowered Christian Ministries in Ejisu (the Ashanti Region Coordinator of Fruitful Ministries) was the smart errand person that ran around to do all the medical and other purchases for us in Kumasi. He was on the ministry team to Brong Ahafo, Northern, and Upper East Regions of Ghana for the missions trip when tragedy struck at Tamale, and **was the one who stood by my hospital bed praying and communicating throughout the night in Tamale**. He even refused to sit down when I asked him to do so, and stood praying through the night while I rolled in excruciating pain in my hospital bed.

When my wife Henrietta heard the description of my condition on phone, and sensed in her spirit what was really at stake, she quickly made phone calls to Dr. Wilson Awasu (our spiritual father in the Lord) in Minnesota, and other friends and ministry partners in California, Ohio, Maryland, and New Jersey to engage in intercession for us. A beloved daughter in the Lord, Charlotte Annor, and her husband Charles in Maryland, informed many Christians and solicited for much prayer in churches in Maryland and Northern Virginia, and I was later told by that the message spread to many churches in the area and a lot of prayers went up to God on my behalf.

After we returned to the USA, Pastor Philip Amofa of Revival Baptist Church in Alexandria, Virginia, told me: "We seriously interceded on your behalf in church and on our Prayer Chain, and we therefore regard your healing and deliverance as one of our huge testimonies of God's answer to our prayers." My wife's cousin Julienne and her husband Thomas Nortey, along with their fellowship members in Charlotte, North Carolina, engaged in intercessory prayers for us.

Henrietta also informed a church where we fellowship, Pastor Tony Clarke and the prayer team of Calvary Chapel in Newport News, Virginia, to intercede for us, and they persisted in aggressive prayers until we returned to the US, and even called us in Ghana for updates in order to pray for us effectively.

A beloved friend (Dr. Barbara Entsuah) belonging to our group Joyful Way Associates, and her husband Joseph Entsuah (one time President of the Inter-Halls Christian fellowship at KNUST in Kumasi around 1980 when I was a biology graduate student on the campus), quickly sent messages to Joyful Way Associates around the world for prayer after receiving the information from Henrietta through a brother at the airport on her way to Ghana. Barbara also encouraged a beloved sister Katie Danso Dankwa in Richmond (Virginia) to call for prayer, who also did a good job of sending messages to her network of prayer partners in the US and Europe to begin praying for me. A beloved sister of Joyful Way Incorporated told us how Joyful Way Inc. members in the present active group seriously interceded for me at their prayer meetings in Accra, Ghana.

My friend Dr. George Manful who ministered close with me as the President of the Inter-Halls Christian Fellowship at KNUST while I was the secretary in 1975/76, encourage my heart when he told me that during a visit to Ghana, he heard about my illness from a nursing sister at Komfo Anokye Hospital, and was so burdened that he fasted for three days to intercede on my behalf.

Our friend Dr. Stephen Ampofo (old schoolmate of KNUST, Kumasi) launched into serious intercessory prayers with Dr. Emmanuel Kwame obeng and their prayer group in New Jersey. Dr. Ampofo regularly called in Kumasi and in Accra to check on my status for specific prayers, and later told me "Our prayer group really went on our knees seriously on your behalf here in New Jersey."

The President of the Ghanaian Association of Hampton Roads in our area (my wife is the present vice President), informed members to pray on our behalf.

The leader of the "Prayer Watch Ministry" in New York City, Rev. Ebenezer Annor (whom I taught biology when he was in secondary school) and his team of prayer warriors, including the Senior Pastor of Ghana Presbyterian Church in Brooklyn, New York (Rev. Sam Atiemo), launched into aggressive prayer for me based upon continuous updates on my health. They still continued to pray for us during and after my initial recovery.

The Fruitful Women (the ladies who help me to organize the Annual Women's Conference in Kumasi, Ghana, and help in ministry to females) engaged in aggressive prayers, sent prayer messages around, and held special prayer meetings to specifically pray for me as well on the campus of KNUST. Their leader, Dr. Mrs. Patience Fleischer, later told me that they were receiving revelations of dead body and coffin at the beginning of their prayer sessions, but as they kept interceding, they started seeing visions of me recovered and healthy, and were assured that I would finally come through successfully.

A beloved old time daughter in the Lord, Mabel Quakye, and her church prayer team in Accra, launched into fervent prayers on our behalf, after they heard at Kaneshie (Accra) Presbyterian Church that sudden illness had prevented me from coming over to minister as originally planned.

A beloved senior Christian brother (Rev. Dr. Theophilus B. Dankwa) in Accra contacted several other senior Christian brethren in and outside Ghana (including leadership and old members of Ghana Scripture Union) to be in serious prayer for me. Mr. Jude Hama (then General Secretary of Ghana Scriputre Union), Rev. John Owusu Afriyie (the well-known Youth

Evangelist, and old time Traveling Secretary of Ghana Scripture Union), and Rev. Nii Amu Darku (former Senior Pastor of Grace Baptist Church in Kumasi, and later Member of the Council of State of the Republic of Ghana) mentioned to me that they (and other colleagues) prayed fervently on my behalf. Mrs. Grace Ababio (wife of Rev. Dr. Isaac Ababio, founder of the Hour of Visitation Choir and Evangelistic Association) called us in Accra during the initial recovery period and encouraged us to know that they had originally received the urgent message from Rev. T. B. Dankwa, and had been in serious prayers for us.

All the churches and ministries plus their pastors and leaders that were left for me to visit on my mission trip but could not do so in Accra, Takoradi, Koforidua, Akuse etc. in Ghana, launched into aggressive prayers on our behalf.

Several other prayer warriors swung into prayer for us, and some followed up with visits to our home while I was recovering in Accra, and in Hampton. Rev. Seth Asante, Rev. John Ofori, and Rev. Osafo Akoto, who were Head Pastors of the Church of Pentecost districts in Maryland, Northern Virginia, and Richmond (Virginia), paid a special visit to us in in our home Hampton.

Mr. Edward Obeng (Presiding Elder of the Church of Pentecost in Albany, New York), who testifies that it is his encounter with me in his High School days in Ghana (Okuapeman Secondary School in Akropong, Akuapem) around1980, that turned his life around when I preached at an evening service in his school (when I was crisscrossing Ghana as a student evangelist), drove all the way for hundreds of miles from Albany (New York) with his wife Agnes to visit us in Hampton, Virginia, and drove back to Albany the same day. That is an example of true love on display.

Beloved ones took it upon themselves to make some announcements on JOY 99.7 FM in Accra and on LUV 99.5 in Kumasi for prayer, and many people sent e-mails, text messages, telephone calls, church announcements, word of mouth at the workplace and in homes etc. for prayer and encouragement. Intensive prayers went on by churches, prayer groups, men and women of God, old and young accompanied by phone calls and support, in several corners of Ghana.

Honestly speaking, we were very much overwhelmed by the national and worldwide demonstration of love, care, compassion, and true spirituality for us. One beloved daughter in the Lord, Mary Yawson (one time President of the Nurses Christian Fellowship at Komfo Anokye Hospital in Kumasi, Ghana) told me later: "The way things were going, I thought I might lose you." Her focus was not even on asking God to just heal me, but said: "In my desperation, I kept telling God all the time that I couldn't afford to lose you."

Many people tell me that they were really scared about my situation, but trusted God as they prayed. One young graduate who is a Christian brother with a lot of love and zeal for the Lord, and is very fond of me, told me: "When your condition was prolonging and no healing seemed to be taking place, I thought to myself that it appears that commitment to God is a life and death matter, when I thought of other men of God as well as dear children of other ministers of the gospel that we had recently lost. But your healing has brought me much relief and hope again."

God loves us and seeks to work on our behalf in all situations. But the Lord chooses to demonstrate His love and power through people who are yielded to His Spirit's leading, seek to live daily by God's will, make every effort to demonstrate sincere love, make themselves available to be used, desire to walk according to God's direction, and have a passion for the fulfillment of God's purposes.

The names of people who prayed and lamented on our behalf or demonstrated compassion are too many to recount, and it is also impossible to know all the people and groups that actually prayed, and so it is better for me not to list too many names and end up leaving some important people out. My wife tells me: "Mention names only when necessary, because you didn't even have the focused mind and means to know most of what went on around you. Some people even came to visit and pray for you when you were sleeping without seeing them, and other lamented for you in little corners in their homes and offices or churches without your knowledge."

The truth is: You know yourselves, and God knows you. That is what is most important. Your reward for your love and prayers is with the Lord. You will receive some of the blessings on earth, but the greatest part of your reward is waiting for you in Heaven. We pray that God will richly bless you, for the sacrifices and the love you demonstrated by praying on our behalf.

CHAPTER SIX

THE VALUE OF A TRUSTED, DEDICATED, AND PRAYING WIFE, AND LOVE OF FAMILY

"Be strong, my dear one. Be strong and don't give up. Try to be strong at least for me, and also for the family".

Those were special encouraging words spoken by my wife Henrietta on our home phone to me before she left the USA to see me in Ghana in August 2009. It was a very tense atmosphere in my home at that time, with no certainty as to what the future was holding.

All along, I felt the compassion for my wife and family, because when a beloved family member suffers, loved ones round the person suffer too; sometimes even more than the victim. Some people died and left more problems and suffering for their spouses and family members more than what the departed one suffered. I knew that it must have been hard and torturous for my wife in her mind and heart, as she tried to figure out what was happening, and when deliverance would come.

She recently mentioned to me as we discussed this manuscript (May 2011), how she looked through a nearby window as she waited behind the door for me to come out of the toilet at Komfo Anokye Hospital in Kumasi in a deeply downcast mode and asked God: "Dear Lord, so, is this where you have brought me on my life's journey?"

I fully understood her. It gets to a crucial point in life when all that you can see yourself doing is to ask difficult questions, without any answers.

The ordeal I went through clearly demonstrated to me the value of a wife who is a remarkable loving spouse, true companion, and faithful friend. Her own past trials before we married, plus excruciating trials and attacks during the early years of our marriage, had prepared her for testing moments like this.

A HUSBAND CANNOT TRULY SUCCEED WITHOUT THE SUPPORT OF HIS WIFE

The prayers of a wife or husband for the other partner cannot be compared with any other prayers, because your partner is the other half of your body by reason of the marriage bond as instituted by God. No prayers of any man or woman of God can especially replace the prayers of a wife for a husband, no matter how the husband views her. She was given to you as a special helper and supporter to become a blessing to you in an exclusive way (Genesis 2: 18). If you could do it all by yourself as a man and fully succeed, God the Creator would not have given her to you.

Any husband who does not allow, encourage, or promote prayers for him by his wife, is missing a lot. No matter how you think you are succeeding as a man in this world, your works will never have the full eternal and spiritual credits and approval before God if you do not perform your God-ordained role of being the priest of your home and helping your wife to develop into a godly woman of prayer and obedience to God's word.

For every extensive mission trip to Ghana or any other country, just before we leave home for the airport, we read the scriptures and pray together. I will typically open Joshua 1: 1-9, and emphasize verse nine: *"The Lord your God is with you wherever you go"*. Then I would thank her for her love, prayers, and care for me which supports my entire life and for the ability to successfully undertake such trips. We would then go through our traditional routine of holding our hands to pray. We often sing a devotional song, after which I always let her pray first, followed by my prayer. On some occasions during our prayer before leaving the house to the airport, I knelt in front of her and asked her to lay her hand on my head, and pray for me for safety and for a productive trip.

HER PRAYERS WITH THE FAMILY AND COMING OVER TO CARE FOR ME

My wife and daughter Hannah told me how they aggressively cried loudly to the Lord for His divine intervention when they learned that I was hospitalized in the Intensive Care of a hospital, and a chest tube had been inserted into my chest cavity, and copious creamy and viscous fluid was constantly exuding from my thoracic cavity into a bottle. Only the two of them were at home at that time, and they told me that our neighbors might have heard them crying out in prayer.

Our son Victor was at work, and they called to give him the grim news. He was jolted by the news, and immediately asked for permission to leave for home. When he arrived they told him he could have stayed till closing time, but he found it necessary to come home and join the family to deliberate, pray and hope for the best.

My wife told me she would go to work (Eastern State Hospital in Williamsburg, Virginia), and sit down in a terribly lifeless and confused state, unable to focus and do any meaningful work. Her colleagues began to encourage her to plan and leave to come over to see me in Ghana. She began to inquire from Dr. Ken Abboa (Chief Surgeon of Komfo Anokye Teaching Hospital) if it was really necessary for her to come over, and finally his wife Mrs. Victoria Abboa convinced her to ask for a leave of absence, and travel to see me. It was a tremendous blessing for me that she finally came over.

Henrietta appeared surprisingly one Tuesday evening (4th August, 2009) at the Intensive Care Unit of Komfo Anokye Hospital in Kumasi (about a week after my admission). She knew that I would not be in favor of her coming down to Ghana (primarily because of the expenses involved), therefore Dr. Ken Abboah and his wife in particular who arranged for her coming kept it as a secret from me.

I looked over on my left from my hospital bed that evening and there was my dear wife! My heart jumped, and I spontaneously asked: "What are you doing here!?" She replied: "But what are you also doing here!?" **She then came close to give me a hug, looked into my eyes and emphatically said to me: "I am NOT accepting this one! You are NOT going to die!"**
She thus spoke faith into me and into my situation. Every wife must emulate this shining example, and desist from grumbling, blaming, and scolding her husband in the face of trying situations.

HER SUPPORT IN THE HOSPITAL AND HER TRUST IN GOD

Henrietta's love, sacrifices, compassion, intense care, application of wisdom, and assistance in and outside of the hospital were phenomenal. Later she told me how she sometimes did not sleep but virtually prayed through the night at home, after bidding me good night in the hospital to go and rest for the night.

Up to now she narrates her experiences in surrendering her will to God as a testimony to encourage people. For example, during a Bible study in our home on Saturday 9th April, 2011, one Christian sister and another Christian Brother brought out a lesson to us regarding the need to surrender all of your will to God during prayers in critical situations. My wife responded with an emphatic statement: "When my husband was seriously ill in Ghana last two years, I got to a point when I could not eat or sleep, and could not focus properly because I had stretched out all of my faith in prayer to the Lord but his situation was not changing. So One day I decided to surrender everything into God's Mighty Hands for Him to do what seemed best and right for Him to do. From that day onwards I started to have my peace, and rested in my spirit as I still communicated with God in faith and waited for Him to see what He was going to do in His infinite wisdom and power. In the end God glorified His Name."

The real value of a great, godly, God-given wife was vividly portrayed to me!

She often employed her nursing skills to ensure the best care from the nurses on duty, ensured the application of aseptic techniques, and was sometimes even allowed to perform some of the procedures on me. At the Kumasi ICU, there was a particular afternoon when the only nurse on duty had to leave for an assignment for about an hour, and she assumed the responsibility as the nurse on duty for all the patients (5 of us in the ICU ward).

Henrietta told me that when she came every morning at 6am to be by my side the whole day and saw fluid still draining from my chest to fill the bottle, she felt discouraged just as I was, but we kept our hopes high. When she left me in the hospital at night to the True Vine Guest House in Kumasi, she often cried at night alongside her prayers, but in all cases, she NEVER told anyone that called to ask about me that I was not improving, but always told the one I was fine and doing okay (as an act of faith), and that they should continue to pray for me.

When the final diagnosis was made, and the doctors told me they needed to open my chest region and deal with the problem, I got a little scared and quite concerned that I was going to be subjected to general anesthesia for hours. Henrietta (being an experienced nurse) did her best to calm me down, and was rather more composed and pleased with the solution to the key problem than I was. He first words were: "Oh, the procedure is not as frightening as you think. Don't be afraid. You will be alright." I actually felt very much encouraged by her attitude and words.

She persuaded me to yield to the physiotherapy team whose exercise drills I hated during their visits to me in the hospital.

She originally requested for one month leave of absence, but when she saw the state in which I was, she decided to stay with me up till 16th October 2009 when we finally left Ghana to the United States after two months.

THANKFUL FOR HER ASSISTANCE IN MY WEAK STATE

Until we came to the USA, she had to assist me in having a bath — I was too weak to do it on my own. In the heat of affairs, she had to even coax me to eat or feed me (I could eat very little).

I had lost so much muscle, and my thighs had become so thin that I saw them as almost the same size as my calf. I joked that I would rank very well alongside one of the people forcibly imprisoned and tortured by starvation as we see in photos shown on television. My legs had little muscle, and the skin was so close to the bones that when I lay down and rested one leg on another, I had to put a pillow between my legs because my knees and feet bones were hurting when the bones touched very closely without any cushion of muscle in between.

I was too weak to put on my own socks or shoes, or even under wears and other attire. I dared not try to kneel down because there was no energy and enough muscles in my legs to help me get up.

When I chewed food or anything, I would often pause after moving my jaws a couple of times in order to rest and gain enough strength and continue chewing. At the beginning of the recovery period food was attractive to me, but having the appetite to consume was the problem. Most often I would try to eat and be in a hurry to partially finish the little amount of food placed before me. Sometimes I even painfully went through the ordeal of consuming and swallowing the food and hoped for the quick end of the eating process, after which I quickly uttered: "Oh, good riddance!", and then left the table. My wife and I would usually laugh at the whole episode.

One Frightening Moment

On Thursday 1st October 2009, I began to feel very dizzy at the end of my dinner. I then got up to visit the bathroom, and the dizziness increased. This was quickly followed by a blackout whereby everything became black for about five minutes. I was deeply concerned, not knowing the cause of the situation and kept repeating: "I have life, in Jesus! I have life, in Jesus!" Henrietta stood before me and kept asking me if she should send me to the emergency room. I told her to hold on while I kept calling on the Lord and saying "I have life in Jesus!" My vision began to clear after a while and I began to feel fine. The power of God was again manifested through the Name of Jesus in prayer and confession of my faith in God's trusted promise. Yes, I have life in Jesus! Hallelujah!

Frequently as well as sporadically, as she gave me a bath, cleaned me, dressed me up, gave me food and medication, I looked into the eyes of my wife and said to her: "Thank you!", or "God bless you!" with a smile", and she always responded with welcome words and a smile.

CARE AND FAMILY ENCOURAGEMENT BACK IN THE USA

When we returned to the USA, she assisted me to have my bath for the first week after which I began to learn how to gradually bath on my own until I gained enough strength to become independent of her assistance. She took time off from her work to accompany me during all of my initial visits to our Primary Care Physician and three other specialists (Surgeon, Infection Specialist, and Lung Specialist).

One day I was in the bathroom when my daughter Hannah came around and said to me in delight: "Daddy, do you know that there is one thing I admire about you?" I asked her what it was, and she replied: "I admire you because you wanted to live. You determined not to die." I was overwhelmed by her remark, and simply kept quiet. On another occasion she came close to me and quoted for me Joel 2:25: *"God will restore to you the years that the locusts have eaten."*

Children must show their gratitude to their parents and guardians, and learn how to speak life and encouraging words to their parents, guardians, and elders, without being always at the receiving end of getting every resource from adults without giving anything back.

It is a real joy and tremendous encouragement as a husband and a father to lead your family in the paths of righteousness and spiritual disciplines of God. In the end your works come back to reward you with prayers, sharing of scripture, encouragement, guidance, support, and family love plus genuine care.

CHAPTER SEVEN

LIFE BACK HOME IN THE USA

GETTING READY TO RETURN TO THE USA

Two days before leaving Korle-Bu Hospital, Dr. Mark Tettey (one of the leading surgeons who did the operation) advised that I stayed home and recovered for at least one month before thinking of flying back to America. I replied that I believed two weeks after I had been discharged, I should be feeling quite fine, and I would like us to return to the USA. He immediately squeezed his face and emphatically remarked: "Oh no! You don't want to stress yourself and put your body through any hardships. Your lungs have to be stabilized too. When you go home, search the Internet for "Boerhaave Syndrome", and you will see what trauma you experienced, and the stressful processes your body had to go through to keep you alive."

Indeed he was right. We fixed the date of departure three weeks away from the date of discharge, but had to postpone for another week because of serious chest infection that set in while at home, with accompanying cough that constantly brought out purulent copious phlegm with varieties of greenish and yellowish colors. We had to re-visit the hospital for tests, and at a medical lab in town, plus CT Scan at Korle-Bu Hospital for detailed investigations on my lungs. I remember being so weak that walking and even sitting for long periods were a pain and big burden.

THE FLIGHT BACK HOME

Finally we prepared to leave, and got our belongings together. My doctor had to give me the all-clear permit that my lungs had been stabilized, and would not collapse in mid-air. My wife was excited and very grateful to God, and bought some white cloth with black designs that she used to sew celebration costumes for us to wear on the plane to the USA. At Kotoka International Airport in Accra, the airport personnel assisted me to the plane in a wheelchair, and we informed the flight crew about my state, and the need to get some oxygen ready in case I needed it.

We managed to successfully go through the 11 hours Delta Airlines flight from Accra to New York City, and one and a half hours flight from

New York City to Norfolk, Virginia (next door to Hampton). There was the apprehension of how my little strength was going to allow me to sit for so many hours, plus any possibilities of lung problems that will necessitate oxygen supplies at some high altitudes. But things worked out well without bothering the pilot and crew who were worried that I was going to deplete their oxygen supply on the plane. They got the oxygen ready, but I did not even use any oxygen at all.

While we were airborne, pain was well managed, with a pain patch attached to my body (that controlled pain in my body for 24 hours — the same as was attached to my back when the ambulance transported me from Kumasi to Accra on August 22nd 2009). My mind was also conditioned for pain, partly because I had experienced so many different kinds of pain that it was no more news to me. The rest of the real bodily pains set in the next 2 days after arrival.

We could not afford the first class that gives more space to relax, but the flight attendants positioned me at the front seat of the economy class where I would get more leg room. Frequent sipping of the nutritious energizing drink Lucozade on the flight, prayers, scriptures, faith, hope, and God's grace enabled us to safely arrive in the USA. My wife sat observantly and prayerfully by my side, and had all of my medications in her handbag that she gave to me at the appropriate times. Transportation in wheelchairs also helped on the ground.

At JFK Airport in New York City, I was being pushed by airport assistance personnel in a wheel chair with Henrietta by my side when we heard a man's loud voice: "God bless you oooo! God bless you! Thank God you are back! The news made us quite scared, but we prayed fervently! Thank God for answering prayers!" We turned and saw that it was an old time good friend Rev. Sam Atiemo, Senior Pastor of the Ghana Presbyterian Church in Brooklyn, New York, who was at the airport to welcome someone.

EVALUATION BY DOCTORS -- DISCOURAGEMENT THAT GAVE WAY TO HOPE

My wife took time off to accompany me on all of my initial hospital visits. A week after our arrival I was examined by our Family Physician in Hampton, Virginia, Dr. Olie Adcock. He expressed much appreciation for the good work done by the Ghanaian Doctors to help me survive and go through the horrible ordeal. He narrated that he had seen an esophageal rupture through vomiting only once in his lifetime when he was in Medical College. One friend had an experience of Boerhaave Syndrome that was discovered two hours after it occurred. Even then he stayed in the hospital for three months after surgery before being discharged. He added: "You are really lucky to be alive!"

Dr. Adcock referred me to Dr. Moy (surgeon with 25 years experience, Sentara Medical Center, Hampton, VA) for surgical follow-up. He remarked to me: "The Good Lord had been good to you, and caused you to be alive. Do you know that 80% of the people who get the problem that you had, never survive?"

I was also examined by Dr. Chugurapati (pulmonary specialist, Hampton, VA), and she commented: "You must be fortunate and lucky to be alive, because many of the people with your kind of problem never make it alive, and we lose them all the time." He explained that my chest region had been so disturbed that unless any of the specialists had to go in there to correct a major problem, none of them would want to put an instrument to my chest at all for any surgical procedure.

Dr. Kluger (infectious disease specialist, Newport News) did his investigations on me to ensure that all of my infections were gone, and he also commented: "You are very fortunate to be alive."

A month after his first examination, I felt confident to drive to the hospital alone, so I asked my wife to go to work and leave me to go to the clinic on my own. Our family physician examined me again and took and X-ray that seemed to indicate the presence of some fluid accumulation around my left lung. That alarmed me quite a bit, and he scheduled me to see the other specialists for their opinion.

On my way home a scary thought came into my mind that if there was a leakage around my lung, then I could not wait for any scheduled visits, and I should rather drive straight to the emergency room. I started experiencing feelings of discouragement, but prayed, rebuked the enemy and refused to allow any fear or doubts and discouragement to overpower me. I had collected copies of Our Daily Bread devotional booklets to distribute in homes in the area on my way home, and rather began to have the thought of coming home to schedule an immediate appointment with my lung, surgical, and other specialists. After a few minutes, courage and hope from God were infused into me, and I parked my car by the roadside within our estates, and got out to share my booklets. That was the first day I drove after we returned from Ghana, and my first time to walk outside for a considerable period as well.

It was cold in the winter as well in late November, but I enthusiastically did my evangelistic activity for about 30 minutes from house to house. Interestingly enough, I saw a car coming as I crossed the road at one point to an opposite home, and was so caught up in what I was doing that I did not bother to find out whose car it was, but drew back for the car to pass. Surprisingly that car slowed down and gradually began to stop. I asked myself "why is this driver behaving like this?" Then I looked up and there was my wife coming from work! We both laughed. I knew that she would be concerned about me walking in the cold with my lung problem and body pains, but I assured her I was almost done with my ministerial activity and would drive home soon. That was good exercise for me as well. I went home rejoicing that the devil did not win; God won!

Since the X-ray alone could not completely tell whether it was a scar tissue that appeared to be fluid collection, the three specialists agreed for me to undergo a 'Barium swallow test' to see if the repaired esophagus was leaking in any way. They also scheduled for me to have a CAT scan which would give them a clearer picture. I was therefore given my first CT scan on December 1st, 2009 to confirm that no fluid had collected around the lungs. As I lay down in the CT scan machine at Sentara Hospital in Hampton Virginia, Psalm 90 came into mind, especially verse 10 that says: *"The days of our lives are seventy years; and if by reason of strength they are eighty years, yet their boast is only labor and sorrow; for it is soon cut off, and we fly away."* I meditated on that scripture and prayed. An hour later the results were sent to the surgeon specialist electronically. He said to me: "Your CT Scan as I see on my computer is good". Only a small pocket of fluid collected within a scar tissue, and he explained that it would be left alone to ultimately disappear without any further surgery. I was still curious, and asked him if the Barium swallow test showed any leakage of the esophagus, and he said "There is no leakage at all". This gave me great relief, because I have to confess that I harbored some fears about a possible leakage after my family physician saw the collection of some fluid from my first X-ray before the CT scan, which made me assume a high level of fluid in my pleural (chest) cavity.

I made a second visit to the infections specialist who confirmed that, after analyzing all the tests that he had conducted his conclusion was that all the infections were gone! Praise God! He, however, made me have a thermometer handy to record my temperature frequently, especially if I felt funny or slightly feverish at anytime. When things begin to go wrong in the body, one of the primary things that happen is the rise of body temperature, since the body defense mechanisms would go into operation to fight the infection. He instructed me to hurry to his clinic without any appointment at anytime that I recorded my body temperature close to or above 100^{0}F. I monitored my temperature for a while in December 2009 and January 2010 but stopped after that until now that I am writing this account (May 2011) without any need to rush anywhere for medical attention because of fever resulting from any complications in my body. Thank you Jesus!

CHAPTER EIGHT

GOD'S WAY OF HEALING

"Jesus said 'This sickness is not unto death'" (St. John 11: 4). "He (Jesus) Himself took our infirmities and bore our sicknesses (diseases)" (Mathew 8: 17).

We need to know and understand that sickness, illness, and diseases are results of the fall of man, and have become part of human weakness and decay. Simply stated, sin brought disease upon mankind.

It is God's will and divine plan to heal and restore us to complete health in Christ in order for us to do and accomplish His will, and therefore many sicknesses are not expected or intended to (or supposed to) end in death (as Jesus Himself emphasized in St. John 11: 4). We can therefore be healed over and over again when we get sick, except "the last sickness" IF God, in His wisdom, decides to allow you to depart out of this world through that particular infirmity.

Since we never fully know the mind of God, our duty is to live in faith and obedience, take very good care of ourselves, do all we can to prevent any diseases or sicknesses from attacking us, and trusting God for full healing when we become sick at anytime.

After all, as we get older, our organs and tissues become old, less functional, or even completely nonfunctional and no more whole or sound, which can be better interpreted as sick and ill. At some stage in our old age the heart, brains, and rest of the organs and the entire body simply give up living anymore. Healing implies sound health, or total wholeness without flaws, infections, imperfections, or destroyed and removed or compromised parts. Most people think of healing as mostly freedom from physical diseases, illness, and infirmities, but healing could be physical, spiritual, emotional, mental, financial, and social.

QUESTIONING GOD?

Have you ever questioned God as to why He delays in healing someone or your own disease? Have you questioned and been baffled by any kind of sickness or illness lingering for a long time and never getting healed? I want to assure you that you are not swimming alone in this sea of dilemma and perplexity.

What you should get deeper into your mind, heart, and spirit, and become absolutely convinced about is the fact that it is God's will for you to live, know God through the acceptance of Jesus Christ as your Savior and Lord, worship and serve God faithfully, bear fruit to the glory of God, and **ultimately fulfill your destiny.**

As a botanist and ecologist, I was elected to be one of the Directors of the Hampton Land Conservancy, which is the first ever conservation organization for the city of Hampton, Virginia, aimed at helping to preserve the green areas that are left in the city. The other Board Members knew about my illness and collectively signed a card and mailed to my home. When I arrived in the US in October 2009 and was able to attend the next meeting in January 2010, they were excited to see me again and very happy that I was able to go through the ordeal, by God's grace. I had not given them any details of how I felt or my reactions and responses to the tragedy, but one of them (Sally, a school teacher) made a wise comment that stuck in my mind. She said: "Sam it is good that you held on to your faith and did not give up. Some people do not finally make it through, and pass away because they struggle with the pain and unexpected situation and give up in their minds and hearts." All the other board members responded in agreement.

Please do not give up too soon! **You may not see the Hand of your Heavenly father at work, but can still trust His heart.**

I have often said that if we could always explain God and understand all of His ways, then He will not be big enough to be God. No matter the circumstances under consideration, we must understand and believe that everything God does is intertwined with His love, mercy, justice and grace. God is never too late or too early, and life holds no surprises at all for Him, because He knows the end from the beginning, and therefore knows all the intervening steps.

With his permission, I decided to quote a portion of an e-mail sent to me by a beloved Christian friend, ministry partner, and school mate in the university, Mr. Bijou Doe in Accra, Ghana, and the current Chair of the Board of Directors of our ministry (Fruitful Ministries International Incorporated). After we arrived in the USA I sent out mail to update people on my condition. He wrote back: *"As I read the details you gave in your mail, I am in tears right now. As we prayed for you I kept wondering why God did not give you an instant miracle on the hospital bed, and you had to suffer for that length of time."*

71

My friend's comment made me remember some stages when I even had to find out which pain to choose from as the pain for that period, and take steps to manage. People often found me lying down in special positions, but many did not know that for each hour of the day, I choose to place myself in the best position that make me feel the least pain in my body. I recall one morning at about 2 am at Korle-Bu Hospital in Accra when there was the usual pain in my chest region from the surgery, then one at the tip of my pelvis (coccyx) from lying on my back for weeks, and an excruciating pain that suddenly surfaced in my right hip joint which was strangely dominating all the other pains, such that it became my focus, and no position I chose to lie down in the bed could make me feel less pain. I just struggled and prayed and moaned for at least two hours until the pain subsided a little bit around 4 am. None of the pain medications I had been given could take that pain away, and I could also not just swallow more medicine until a specific time had elapsed for the next dose of medicine.

Does it mean God did not love me enough to listen to my prayer and immediately take away that sudden pain which was an unnecessary addition to the other pains I was already having? No; not at all! The Lord was right there in my pain.

When the greatest Apostle, Paul, had a thorn in his flesh (a form of affliction) and prayed fervently for God to deliver him from it, God did not answer his prayer they way he expected, but used the affliction to humble and strengthen him spiritually. Paul learned to be more dependent on God, and developed the understanding for the value of afflictions and infirmities, if God allows them to be in your life for any length of time.

"And lest I should be exalted above measure by the abundance of the revelations, a thorn in the flesh was given to me, a messenger of Satan to buffet me, lest I be exalted above measure. Concerning this thing I pleaded with the Lord three times that it might depart from me. And He said to me: 'My grace is sufficient for you, for My strength is made perfect in weakness.' Therefore most gladly I will rather boast in my infirmities, that the power of Christ may rest upon me. Therefore I take pleasure in infirmities, in reproaches, in needs, in persecutions, in distresses, for Christ's sake. For when I am weak, then I am strong" (2 Corinthians 12:7-10).

WHAT IS DELIVERANCE?

I wish to comment that deliverance (one of the most popular words in our time and in Christianity) is not a one way street as several people make us believe. The major impression is that deliverance simply means being set free completely from a problem, unfavorable situation, bad habit or spiritual condition (oppression, possession, obsession, deception).

My understanding is that deliverance is in two forms:

1) **Delivered <u>from</u> the situation.** In this case the problem goes away and you are rescued out of it completely.

2) **Delivered <u>through</u> the situation.** In this case you will still have to go through the problem for a season in order for God to teach you some important lessons, become humbled, get strengthened in your faith, and toughened in your character, and finally come out of it on the other end of the dark tunnel leaving the problem behind you.

David knew this secret and said: *"Yea, though I walk through the valley of the shadow of death, I will fear no evil; For You are with me; Your rod and Your staff, they comfort me"* (Psalm 23: 4).

David did not say "I will not know or will not see any evil."

We therefore have to be extra careful how we use our experiences or experiences of others and what we read or hear as testimonies to judge others who have prayed or exercised faith, or whom we have prayed for and believed God with, but are still struggling with their illnesses and problems.

Sometimes I wonder how some people felt when I was lying helplessly in the hospital bed in Kumasi for one month with no sign of improvement after all the prayers and faith of loved ones and churches had been exercised. None of us even knew what was really happening to me to even pray specifically during that period.

STRETCHING OF OUR FAITH

On some occasions in the hospital in Kumasi, I tuned myself to exercise my faith as much I could, and prayed for God to touch and heal me. I remember one day when I imagined the source of the issuing fluid totally drying up when I got up in the morning, and becoming completely healed. Then I further imagined the news appearing in the newspapers under the caption: "Miracle at Komfo Anokye Teaching Hospital!"

But as deep or strong as my convictions and expectations were, that did not happen, and I saw the fluid filling the jar connected to the chest tube every morning. I did not share these thoughts with anyone, and kept them to myself asking and listening to God for explanations without positively knowing why God would not perform the quick miracle I expected.

I knew that my wife believed God along with me in the same direction, and sometimes both of us were disappointed when she came in the early morning for us to examine the container and found it almost full with the fluid. Sometimes when that happened we together quietly muttered "Oh Lord". But we still held on to our faith in God to finally break through for us.

WHY DOES GOD DELAY IN HEALING, OR DOES NOT HEAL AT ALL?

This scripture will give us some insights into the answer to this question: *"The Lord your God will drive out those nations before you little by little; you will be unable to destroy them at once, lest the beasts of the field become too numerous for you"* (Deuteronomy 7:22).

If you do not receive instantaneous healing for your illness, or victory for your trial, be encouraged to rest your heart in the comfort that God's resounding victory is sometimes little by little, along with His wisdom, until your victory is complete.

I have pondered over, thought through, keenly observed, and added all my findings and ideas to personal experiences and will want to confidently suggest the following reasons for delays in healing (plus deliverance, or restoration) processes, and cases where everything remains unchanged or gets partially alright:

1) **God might want to get better and greater glory.** An example is the case for Lazarus when he died. If Jesus had hurried to the place to heal him it would have been wonderful, but He delayed till Lazarus died, and obtained better glory and greater joy for the family and friends. *"Now Martha (sister of Lazarus) said to Jesus, 'Lord if you had been here, my brother would not have died. But even now I know that whatever You ask of God, God will give you'"* (St. John 11:21, 22). Jesus finally came out to tell her: *"Did I not say to you that if you believe you would see the glory of God?"* (St. John 11:40).

2) **The extended periods of prayers deepen our fellowship with God.**
God delights to interact closer and deeper with us in sweet and intimate fellowship, which comes only through much prayers and meditation on God's goodness and His word in His Presence.
Isaiah 40:30, 31.

3) **Godly character is built in us in the process.**
Our joy and peace plus guidance and specific directions and instructions become clearer through the waiting, prayers, and meditation. We gain better understanding of suffering, and learn new ways of overcoming trials and living victorious lives.
James 1:12; Hebrews 12: 11.

4) **Our faith grows and becomes stronger.**
The fires of affliction refine our faith, and the various aspects of the entire exercise teach us valuable lessons that make us trust God more for greater future needs.
James 1:2-4; 1 Peter 1:3-9.

5) **We are humbled to become more dependent upon God.**

There is nothing that cuts through the ego and pride of our humanity and brings us on our knees to surrender and yield fully to God, than sickness, illness, or afflictions and disappointments that temporarily incapacitate us or halt us in our earthly pursuits. When the severity increases, we become afraid of shame, losses, defeat, prolonged paralysis, failure of our dreams, and even death. We are consequently haunted by the possibility of meeting and facing people who will hold us accountable, and finally facing our Maker. That unexpected stern condition that suddenly confronts us automatically compels us to ponder more on our faith and lifestyle, and think deeper about destiny, success, eternity and judgment, more than ever before. We develop greater dependence on God's grace and mercy, and rely more on God's unfailing promises.
1 Peter 1: 6, 7.

6) **God might be trying to get your attention.**

Sometimes our ears become dull of hearing. Self-confidence or stubbornness slowly creeps into our minds and hearts to make us stiff-necked and rebellious or very casual in the observance of rules and regulations. Disobedience therefore opens wide doors for the enemy to attack us, to the point of being bombarded with failures, assailed by afflictions, or falling ill. The truth is that our iniquities and transgressions can invite discipline and punishment from the Lord that could include diseases and sicknesses. That is why some diseases and illnesses are linked to sin.
"God forgives all your iniquities and heals all your diseases" (Psalm 103:4).
Psalm 119: 67, 92; Exodus 15: 26.

7) **God might be training you to prepare for greater blessings ahead.**

Sometimes we are not ready to receive, preserve, and make the best use of favors, opportunities, gifts, grace, and blessings that God plans to give us to use to his glory, especially when there are bad habits that we adore but are not willing to get rid of. Sometimes the suffering we go through is designed to make us appreciate and empathize with family members and friends, and people we are going to minister to, whom we have to help to deal with their personal afflictions and problems. God has the right and ability plus wisdom to use anything He chooses in His sovereignty to prune, cleanse, and get us ready for success. I dare think and say that different forms and various degrees of sicknesses and illnesses could be part of God's chiseling tools that He may allow (not necessarily bring) into our lives as preparation that will humble, refine and toughen us for proper handling of future opportunities. Finally we will go through our times of testing and refinement and come out as better servants of the Lord.
St. John 15:1-5; Romans 8:18; 2 Corinthians 4:17, 18.

8) God uses affliction to prevent greater disaster.

Have you ever heard people saying that someone had to suffer from an illness or other form of affliction (or even die from a disease or calamity) to prevent or stop more harm to the one and others around? None of us can read the mind of God unless he reveals something to you, but there could be some truth in this. Whatever the case, we must heed to God's warning to be very careful how we flippantly violate or toy with God's holy laws, dabble in witchcraft and occultism, become entrenched in immorality and addictions, refuse to repent and turn away from repeated sins, and take God for granted.

In this respect, a story just came into mind: In 1988 I was a Ph.D. biology graduate student and an adjunct lecturer at Lehman College (City University of New York) in the Bronx. One of my Hispanic undergraduate students who knew I was a Christian and was among students that frequently had conversations with me about spiritual solutions to the issues of life, came to tell me in class, in a tense mood, how a family member had been shot and killed by drive-by shooting. Although she was quite disturbed by the incident, she kept repeating how she had personally warned the boy to keep good company and avoid vengeance, because he had quarrels with some of the gang members in the neighborhood, and had vowed to get back at them. He was so troublesome and so drifted away from things of God to the extent that no amount of advice from parents and other family members would dissuade him to abandon his riotous life with evil company. The parents who were devoted church members and other elderly family members surprisingly prayed that since the boy was too much to handle, and could bring more troubles upon himself and others, God should change him or take him away. Wow! Soon after they started praying that way, he was standing in front of a store when some guys in a car drove by and shot him to death instantly. The girl had just come from the funeral, and narrated the story to me. In the words of my student: "He would not listen to any advice, and God took him."
This seems to go along with what Paul asked the Corinthians to do to a chronic immoral member of the church in Corinth (1 Corinthians 5:4, 5).

9) Some diseases and illnesses demand more power for removal.

There are instances where a sickness or illness is so rooted in a way that demands more prayer and application of God's word for more power of God to be released before healing could take place. This applies to several cases of illnesses with satanic connection. In other words, the disease or sickness could be the result of demonic oppression, and until the evil spirit is cast out or rebuked to leave the person, the illness will prevail and linger on. Jesus dealt with several of such cases.
Luke 9:37-42; Mark 5:1-20.

HOW GOD HEALS AND DELIVERS
"Jesus said to him 'I will come and heal him'" (Mathew 8: 7).

Yes, the Lord wants to come and heal you, but you must cooperate with Him and fulfill your part of the agreement with submission to His will, meditation and application of God's word, obedience, prayer, faith, and complete trust in God's love and power.

One of the reasons why God came down to us as Jesus Christ was to heal us (physically and spiritually). God heals diseases and illnesses, and delivers us from demonic oppression, trials, tragedies, afflictions, dangers, and even death through:

1) Your own personal prayers of faith. You have a general believe God as the Almighty who has love for mankind and is willing to assist us anytime with our needs including healing, and you therefore ask Him to heal you. Mathew 9:27-31; Luke 5:12-14.

2) Your specific personal knowledge of God's power to heal, and appropriation of the knowledge to exercise faith independently by confessing and acting on your faith without involving anyone else. An example is the woman with issue of blood who touched the garment of Jesus in Mark 5: 25-34.

3) God's word and personal Bible studies. Some sicknesses vanish as you seriously study and meditate on scripture. God's word has healing, cleansing, and restoration powers through His Spirit working through His word. *"He sent His word and healed them, and delivered them from their destructions"* (Psalm 107: 20). *"You are already clean because of the word which I have spoken to you"* (St. John 15:3); *"How can a young man cleanse his way? By taking heed according to Your word"* (Psalm 119:9).

4) The prayers and faith of loved ones on your behalf (even when you cannot pray for yourself, including those raised from the dead or who were in a coma or on life support system). James 5:14, 15; Luke 7:11-17; Luke 5:18-26; Mark 1:29-31.

5) Corporate prayers along with other Christians who stand in agreement with you. *"Confess your trespasses (sins) to one another, and pray for one another, that you may be healed. The effective fervent prayer of a righteous man avails much (has great power in its effects)"* (James 5: 16). Also Acts 12:5; Ezra 8:21-23.

6) God's direct touch through His Spirit of healing (without any human involvement). Some diseases have sometimes suddenly vanished from people during worship, singing, or as they listened attentively to sermons or spiritual music. Luke 5:15-17.

7) God's touch or laying of hand through another Christian friend who walks by faith. Mark 16: 17, 18.

8) God's touch or laying of hand through an anointed servant of God with special gift of healing from God. 1 Corinthians 12:9.

CHAPTER NINE

HOW DO YOU DEAL WITH STORMS?

Although you cannot in any way control the storms of life, you can always make your boat strong enough to go through the storms of life successfully.

What do you really do when you believe you are in God's will and doing your best in life, and then a storm hits you unexpectedly along the road of life? How do you effectively handle that particular storm?

DEFINE YOUR STORM

You must always define your storm properly before you can understand what is going on and deal with it effectively. As you sit behind your Bible to meditate, and then analyze the situation in prayer before the Lord, He will tell you what is happening. God still speaks to all of us through Christ (Hebrews 1:1-3). If you still cannot figure out what is going on (which will happen most of the time, at least at the beginning), simply leave matters into God's Hand, and trust that God's love is always intertwined with all of His actions.

The two major categories of storms are:
a) **Correcting storms** — due to disobedience or carelessness, such as the storm that Job faced when he decided to run away from God after being sent by Him (Jonah chapter one).
b) **Perfecting storms** — due to obedience which God wishes to perfect and strengthen your faith for more obedience and greater ministry, by training you through a storm that he allows into your life. Example is the storm faced by the Disciples of Jesus when he instructed them to cross to the other side of the lake in a boat (Mark 6:45-51).

PRINCIPLES FOR HANDLING YOUR STORM

I wish to provide six encouraging principles that you can employ to handle your storm victoriously. Say these to yourself and let them get into your mind, heart, and spirit as you face and fight through your storm.

Caution! You must be within the boundaries of God's will before such confessions will have meaning. If not, then please get out of your sinful or self-will condition in genuine repentance, and be on God's side for Him to help you deal with your storm. Some situations are tough — for example: In case you are outside of God's will, such as "unequal yoke" of a Christian marrying a non-Christian out of disobedience, when God has warned every Child of His NOT to try and "marry light and darkness together", then repent, confess your disobedience, and ask God to tell you what to do next.

In cases of dating and courtship, you have every chance to completely get out of any immoral, adulterous, illegal, incompatible, or unfruitful relationship. Then clean up every trace of dirt or filth in your life through prayer and application of the Blood of Jesus plus the cleansing power of Bible meditation, apply faith to have a clean slate, and start all over again.

If you happen to be divorced, you can dream again, and let God guide you into a fresh future in accordance with the guiding principles of scripture, and in terms of your unique situation. Then study your Bible and follow God's steps. You may have to live with some consequences all the days of our life, but God's love and peace can still be in your life to restore you; and you can still engage in useful service plus worship, once you determine to allow the Holy Spit to fill and control your life from that point onwards.

If you get directly into God's will, or later get back into God's will after a detour, then tell yourself:

1) I am facing a storm that I need to deal with.
Admit you are facing a storm, and say to yourself: "God brought me to this place", or "God allowed me to face this storm for a purpose."

2) God is in charge, and Jesus is praying for me.
When the Disciples were sent out on the lake by Jesus, He departed to the mountain to pray (Mark 6: 45, 46). Jesus constantly prays for us in Heaven. *"He lives to make intercession for us"* (Hebrews 7:25). It is comforting to know that as the disciples struggled with the storm, Jesus was seeing and watching them from the shore (Mark 6:48). The Lord sees and knows all that you are facing.

3) Jesus will come to me.
"I will not leave you orphans; I will come to you" (St. John 14: 18). It does not matter how long it takes, but the Lord will finally come to you in your midst of your storm. **One of the difficulties in a storm is the feeling of loneliness, and the thought or feeling that God does not care.** The same wind

Facing and Fighting Through the Storm

and waves that frightened them also brought Jesus to them to deal with their storm (Mark 6:48-50).

4) The Lord will help me to grow better and stronger.
In Luke 5:1-11, Simon Peter grew stronger in his faith, trusted more in the Lord, and developed deeper commitment after the Lord gave him a breakthrough for his fishing problem.

5) The Lord will see me through.
In all instances, the disciples never perished in any storm as they walked with the Lord in obedience. In Luke 8:22, Jesus told the Disciples: *"Let us cross over to the other side of the lake."* That was a promise from the Lord that they would by all means arrive at the other side of the body of water that formed a barrier (problem) between them and where they needed to go. A storm suddenly erupted, but *"Jesus rose up and rebuked the wind and the raging of the water, and they ceased, and there was calm"* (Luke 8: 24).

6) Jesus is with me here, and I have faith in Him.
"Then Jesus went up into the boat to them, and the wind ceased" (Mark 6:51). *"But Jesus said to them: 'Where is your faith'"* (Luke 8: 25). Allow Jesus to get into your boat that is rocking on turbulent waters, then trust in Him and express your total faith in Him, and all of your winds and waves will finally cease for you to have peace and calm.
"You (God) will keep him in perfect peace, whose mind is stayed on You, because he trusts in You" (Isaiah 26: 3).

CONCLUDING THOUGHTS

"But thanks be to God, who always leads us in His triumph in Christ, and manifests through us the sweet aroma of the knowledge of Him in every place" (2 Cor. 2:14).

GOD'S DELIVERANCE AND PRESERVATION ARE AWESOME!

On 23rd of December 2009, I received an unexpected phone call from Dr. Lawrence Sereboe, the leader of the team of surgeons who operated on me at the Korle-Bu Teaching Hospital on Wednesday 26th August, 2009. He said "Merry Christmas", and asked how I was doing physically. I let him know that I was recovering fast, and doing very well. Then he remarked: "Do you know that what happened to you has never happened to anyone before?" I was somehow taken aback, and responded: "Well, I am not really aware of that. I know that vomiting and rupturing your esophagus (Boerhaave Syndrome in medical language) is a rare condition, but it has happened to a few people worldwide, which the medical community encourages that doctors report cases where the victims survive after 2 days, since the condition is the most fatal of all problems associated with the esophagus (gullet) that connects the throat with the stomach. Most esophageal perforations have been cause by accidental puncturing with surgical instruments or accidental swallowing of bones and other sharp objects."

Dr. Sereboe gave a reply to my question: "That is not exactly what I am referring to. In the medical records of the entire world, the longest-lived person who survived esophageal rupturing or perforation without any immediate medical attention for surgery and treatment was eight (8) days. You survived for one month (24th July to September 26, 2009) before your condition was detected and attended to in an operation theater! We shall make an official report to the medical world!" Wow!

You can imagine how I kept quiet and was absolutely stunned! This is what God can do for His beloved children who put their trust in Him, and especially when they are struck by the enemy and by tragedy in the ministerial field. This is also what God can do for us, when loving people intercede for you in abundance.

GOD'S LOVE IS IMMEASURABLE AND BOUNDLESS

The experiences my wife and I went through, made us see the immeasurable extent of God's love and care for us and our family, and for all of us (Ephesians 3:14-20). A Nursing Sister of Komfo Anokye Hospital (an old daughter in the Lord that I knew in her youthful days in Asanteman Secondary School in Kumasi), visited me often, and frequently made the remark: "We (doctors & nurses) give medication and treatment, but healing comes from God."

I have understood more of the importance of living a gracious and diligent life that looks for opportunities to develop and make the best use of all your talents and gifts to the glory of God, as an integral part of your worship and lifestyle, in order to fulfill your destiny.

As I mentioned before, when I was a zealous young Christian in the university doing extensive evangelism, I always said that I wished to die during ministry in the battlefield (during the heat of spiritual battle of ministry). I conceived the exuberant notion that it would be an excellent way to die gloriously. After living for a while and going through many experiences, I do not say that anymore, not because it is no more honorable to pass away and be with the Lord that way, but the primary focus now is on living long enough to influence many lives and win hundreds of souls into God's Kingdom, ensuring that I never depart until I have been called home properly by God at anytime.

People's effort to mobilize support for us along with their care, love, prayers, donations, gifts, visits, expressions of compassion, phone calls, e-mails etc. were overwhelming for us. God brought to our attention how much unseen love and support we potentially had in store among our friends, especially Christian brethren.

Each stage of my story taught me valuable lessons of life. I learned the need to be in constant state of preparedness to face every circumstance that God will allow to cross your path in your daily routine.

THE VALUE OF SUFFERING —— WHY DOES GOD ALLOW SUFFERING IN OUR LIVES?

Two major themes that people kept drumming into my ears (and I know they still do) are:

1) "Attacks of the devil and forces of darkness suddenly came into your life to snuff you out because you a threat to the enemy."

2) "God took you through an exceptionally trying experience to make you a testimony to others of His love, grace, power, deliverance, and salvation, in order to use your life to glorify His Name."

Panic And Fear

People have asked me if I was scared and gripped with fear during the ordeal. I know that they wish to know if I was afraid of possible death. To honestly answer that question, I have to admit that I was deeply concerned about my situation and wondered how such an occurrence could suddenly erupt in my life, and what all the events meant.

But, in reality, although I was deeply concerned about the delay in my recovery, I was not significantly scared during the entire period except for three major instances.

The first instance was when I initially vomited and experienced the incredibly sharp pains in my chest at Tamale — I really panicked.

The second occasion was when my stomach churned with some fear immediately I was told by Dr. Lawrence Sereboe at Korle-Bu Hospital in Accra upon the detection of the primary cause of my problem: "we need to open you up; you have a ruptured esophagus that we need to fix".

The third instance that I panicked to a considerable extent was when one evening at the end of my dinner at home, I suddenly started experiencing dizziness which escalated for me to black out with everything looking very dark, and my entire body feeling very sick. When my wife asked me what was wrong, I just kept saying: "Everything looks dark; everything looks black." She stood before me as I sat in a chair in the living room, and asked me if she ought to send me to the emergency room, but I asked her to wait. I kept repeating the words: "I have life in Jesus! I have life in Jesus!" After about 10 minutes, things began to clear for me to see well again, while the sickening fear also subsided. I felt relieved, and thanked the Lord for touching me to rescue me.

It is the Presence of God with us that ultimately cuts through and destroys all of our fears. In all instances I heavily depended on God's Presence with me, and called upon the Name of the Lord for confidence and deliverance, and the Lord faithfully and lovingly heard my cries for His grace and mercy to be in operation.

"Fear not, for I am with you; Be not dismayed, for I am your God. I will strengthen you, Yes I will help you, I will uphold you with My righteous right Hand" (Isaiah 41:10).

"Fear not, for I am with you" (Isaiah 43:5).

FINISHING MY WORK

Considering the level of the illness that hit me so unexpectedly, and the critical near-death experience I had, many people said (and still say) that I have not yet finished my work on earth yet, and that is why God kept me alive.

<u>**Question**</u>: **What work have I not yet finished?**

84

I trust that you will pray along with me to find out and understand more of the unfinished work ahead of me, and how to get that work finished with abundant fruit as God has purposed and commanded for me to accomplish (St. John 15:1-16).

God always wants us to finish what He assigns to us as our task (St. John 4:34). Jesus was waiting till the right moment on the Cross that He could declare: *"It is finished!"* (St. John 19:30), before He could be satisfied to return to his Father because His earthly mission was accomplished.

Rev. Albert Cosmos Ocran of Joyful Way Associates (one of my old sons in the Lord from his secondary school days in the early 1970's, and present Director of Ghana Torchbearers Evangelistic Ministry) visited us at Korle-Bu Hospital in Accra and commented to us and other visitors present: "We have been interceding for you a lot at our ministry office, although you don't even know some of the workers there. If you lose one person who can face the devil and cast out demons, you lose an important component in the Kingdom of God and in Christian ministry."

A beloved Christian brother in Massachusetts (Mr. Mac Obiri Mainoo) remarked to me on phone: "Looking at the entire picture, your experience was clearly one that the enemy intended for death, but God mightily intervened, and the truth is that if we lose a person like you with long term seasoned Christian experience, it takes God a very long time to train and equip someone as replacement."

My Response?

In response to people's comments, I have been saying that I need to know what will of God is there for me to accomplish from now till my final departure. When I said that I now need to wait upon God to find out His will as to why He kept me alive, Mrs. Victoria Abboah (wife of Dr. Ken Abboah of Komfo Anokye Hospital in Kumasi) who was visiting us during my recovery period smiled and remarked: "You are rather in God's will now and that is why the devil is attacking you trying to discourage or destroy you this way!" Hmmm; she set me thinking, and I still ponder over that statement.

I realized also that God used my illness as an opportunity to re-unite with many old students, friends, family members, and disciples in the Lord, and making new friends as well. Several people had the opportunity to show their love and express their compassion. Many were humbled to see how frail and helpless we are as *"grass that grow up and flourish in the morning, and is cut down and withers in the evening"* (Psalm 90: 5, 6).

ULTIMATE BENEFITS OF ILLNESS, TRIALS, AND SUFFERING

"For our light affliction, which is but for a moment, is working for us a far more exceeding and eternal weight of glory" (2 Corinthians 4: 17).

"Now no chastening (discipline) seems to be joyful for the present, but painful; nonetheless, afterward it yields the peaceful fruit of righteousness to those who have been trained by it. Therefore strengthen the hands which hang down, and the feeble knees, and make straight paths for your feet, so that what is lame may not be dislocated, but rather be healed" (Hebrews 12:11-13)

Even the caption of this subtopic must startle, raise a red flag, and appear repulsive to some of you. You may ask: "Is there really any blessing we derive from sicknesses and illnesses? I have already elaborated on the primary reasons why God might delay healing or rescuing you from illness or an undesirable situation. I believe that if we critically examine all the facts, we can understand the concept and accept the truth that there is some form of usefulness and blessings attached to several shapes and forms of illness, trials, and suffering in this world.

For example, the fundamental discipline in the form of imprisonment or hard labor and denial of different kinds of benefits or favors (or even corporal punishment), has been used to straighten criminals, stubborn individuals, violators of the law, or wrongdoers, for the purpose of getting their minds geared towards obedience and righteous living. But people still ask: "How could serious sicknesses and diseases produce any benefits?"

The truth is that God, while **He may not bring the illnesses or diseases, would sometimes allow them to afflict a person** (including God's beloved and devoted children), in order for God to use them as tools to:

1) Humble you, break your pride, and continually keep you in line to do his will to completion.

2) Teach you new lessons you could learn by no other means.

3) Enable you to see and comprehend how frail and weak we are as humans.

4) Make you develop total dependence and trust in the Lord.

5) Build a stronger faith in you.

6) Burn away the chaff and impurities in your life, as fire that refines you.

7) Discipline you for disobedience.

8) Test your loyalty and faithfulness.

9) Enable you to appreciate all of His gifts, and develop a heart of gratitude.

There are varied categories and different intensities of ailments and sicknesses from multiple sources, in accordance with the fall of mankind and human frailty.

REASON FOR LINGERING ILLNESS, AND APPLICATION OF FAITH AND MEDICINE

Some sicknesses are so mild that we can ignore them and may not even have to treat them, since they do not have any significant effect on our health, or distract us from our routines. Other illnesses can knock us down for brief periods after which we become free.

On the other hand, there are a number of diseases and illnesses that are catastrophic, destructive, debilitating, and even potentially lethal, which can impact our health very significantly, and could be chronic throughout our existence.

I notice that no matter what illness or sickness we experience, none of them is welcome or easily accepted because of the discomfort, pain, or other negative results of their effects. Whenever they linger on, we tend to question their presence, and as their seriousness or undesirable consequences progress, we seek for answers as to why we are being afflicted.

Sometimes the source of the sickness or illness is obvious, but in many cases it baffles you and surprises everyone around you as to why and how you got that disease or affliction.

We must know and understand (and admit when we need to) that the devil is secretly behind many sicknesses, diseases, and afflictions, even when an obvious infection sets in. If Job (in the Bible) were with us today, the skeptical, the unbelieving, the disbelievers, and the doubters, including the ignorant, will argue, even when you present them with the truth, and conclude that it is mere infection that has given Job several boils on his body. Any satanic involvement or influence and attack would be totally dismissed. We would rely on our advanced knowledge of scientific and medical innovations and technological applications to deal with what should be first and foremost attacked spiritually by prayer ad scripture, for the devil to be rebuked by faith, before Job would be free.

It is also unwise to despise medicine, since God gives wisdom to mankind for medical discoveries and healing techniques. Those who totally despise taking medicine for any form of sickness or illness are rather unspiritual and unwise.

If God specifically lays it on your heart and clearly tells you NOT to take medicine but only pray for a specific illness, then let it be so. I know some people who are exclusively gifted in that area, and therefore scarcely take medicine, but that is between them and their God. However, I wish to strongly advice you not to copy anyone blindly. Be yourself, and exercise your personal faith in God through Jesus Christ, and hear the Lord speak to you about your situation, because God has spoken to all of us through Jesus (Hebrews 1: 1-3).

If we sincerely wait on the Lord, He might tell us why we have contracted a certain disease, fallen ill, or feel sick (but know also that in many cases you might not get any direct answers from Him). If you get Sexually Transmitted disease (STD) or HIV (AIDS) infection from immorality and sexual perversion, or dress lightly to go out in cold weather and catch a severe cold, then you might not need to ask God why — you should know where it came from, shouldn't you? In that case you must humbly repent and ask God for forgiveness regarding your disobedience or carelessness, and then plead with Him to heal you by faith as you approach God in prayer based upon the mercies of Jesus Christ who paid the penalty for your sins and iniquities on the Cross of Calvary.

This aspect of our discussion is deeper and more complex than these fringes I am tackling, and scratches that I am trying to produce on the surface of the subject. Getting into the complexities will totally take us away from the major theme of this book into other subjects, and I encourage you to seek for good health directives plus Bible-based wise counsel for any health problems that are challenging in your life, and for which you know you contributed towards the problem.

However, if a response comes from the Lord as you seek his face regarding any challenging illness or trial, then it is very likely to fit into one of the nine categories that I have listed above that provide the likely purpose of your condition.

ASSURANCES FROM THE LORD — YOU ARE NOT ALONE IN THIS ONE

"In the days of His flesh, He (Jesus) offered up prayers and supplications, with vehement cries and tears to Him (God the Father) who was able to save Him from death, and He was heard because of His godly fear, though He was a Son, yet He learned obedience by the things which He suffered" (Hebrews 5:7, 8).

We can see that even Jesus Christ our Lord who had no iniquity in His heart had to learn obedience through trials, afflictions, and the accompanied suffering (when he put on a human form to do His father's will). What about me? What about you?

A beloved Welsh Christian lady, living in London, England, who has been a trusted family friend and ministry partner in Europe for several years, wrote to me on June 2nd, 2011: "I don't know if I ever told you, but when you were taken ill—still unknown to me—the Lord directly asked me to pray for you. I assumed it was for the ministry rather than for your survival, but clearly He had the full intention of pulling you through."

Oh yes! Our God is ever faithful. We must always be assured that the will and the love of God will never take any child of God to where His grace cannot keep him or her. **If God brought you to it, then God will take you through it.**

In the event of any illness, epidemic outbreak, breakdown of body tissue due to age, emotional or mental or any other form of sickness, let us pray and cry out with Jeremiah: *"Heal me O Lord and I shall be healed; save me, and I shall be saved, for You are my praise"* (Jeremiah 17: 14).

Let us therefore understand and value the great significance of suffering in any shape and form, as we go through this temporary life to enter our eternal home above.

God knows every detail of all that you have gone through, what you are going through right now, and what you are going to struggle through tomorrow. God feels your pain, and shares your burden with you. *"In all their affliction He was afflicted, and the Angel of His presence saved them; In His love and in His pity He redeemed them; And He bore them and carried them all the days of old"* (Isaiah 63: 9).

So far as you live in humility, faith, and obedience, God promises you: *"When you pass through the waters, I will be with you; And through the rivers, they shall not overflow you. When you walk through the fire, you shall not be burned, nor shall the flame scorch you. For I am the Lord your God, the Holy One of Israel, your Savior. Indeed before the day was, I am He; **And there is no one who can deliver out of My hand. I work, and who will reverse it?**"* (Isaiah 43: 2, 3, 13).

I wish to finally encourage you with this thought:
If you do not at anytime see the Hand of your Heavenly Father working for you, you can still (and always) trust His heart.

Pray as Jeremiah did: *"O Lord, my strength and my fortress, my refuge in the day of affliction"* (Jeremiah 16:19).

And hear Jesus telling you what he told Martha when her brother Lazarus died and had been buried for four days: *"Did I not say to you that if you would believe you would see the glory of God?"* (St. John 11: 40). So, keep believing, keep hoping, and keep serving, and keep living normal life as best as you can in the midst of any sickness and affliction.

89

May the Lord continue to "wash our eyes with tears so that we can see better", whenever the Lord sees the need for us to be taken through the refining process of affliction, for a better view of God Himself, and a clearer view of the road of life on which the road bumps of our pilgrimage are carefully, wisely, and lovingly designed and positioned to break, melt, and mold us into the sparkling and joyful image of Christ, to the glory of God.

*"But may **the God of all grace**, who called us to His eternal glory by Christ Jesus, **after you have suffered a while**, perfect, establish, strengthen, and settle you. To Him be the glory and the dominion forever and ever. Amen"* (1 Peter 5:10, 11). No matter how long it seems to you, God still calls it "a little while."

"For the Lord will be your everlasting Light. And the days of your mourning shall be ended"
(Isaiah 60: 20).

APPENDIX

A) SAMPLE OF TESTIMONY
(Published with permission)

There are several encouraging notes, cards, and mail from people, which will be too voluminous to add to this manuscript. Probably they should be complied into a separate book for motivation. I thought of selecting only one mail as a sample to promote love and encouragement, and to honor the blessings of the Lord that abound as we connect with people, show them genuine love, and minister freely to them. I remember preaching in the church of this lady in Kumasi, Ghana, in the morning of Sunday 27th July 2008 when she had just graduated from medical school, and was called forward to be prayed for. My heart went out to her in compassion (one of the signs of God's leading in ministry).

After the church service I approached her in order to acquaint myself with her, and collect her contact information. She smiled with enthusiasm and told me: "This is interesting and surprising, because as you preached, I told myself that I wish I could know this man and make him my spiritual father. And here you are having the same thought of making me one of your spiritual daughters." So, that was the beginning of a father-daughter relationship. I later learned from her that both her father and mother became ill and died in the same year.

She sent me this mail to me in the USA from Komfo Anokye Teaching Hospital in Kumasi where she works now, and visited my wife and I when I was in the ICU of the hospital in August 2009. When I called her to tell her we are publishing her mail in this book, she laughed and said: "You know what? I started writing this mail to you, but I erased it and left off. Then on another day I started and left it as a draft. I did so at least three times, not being very sure how to craft it to encourage you. I am very glad that it produced an impact just as I wished. She gladly agreed for us to publish it, but was shy to disclose her identity, and was happy when I told her that I had already planned to use only her initials.

I recall one particular night when she visited me at the Komfo Anokye Hospital ICU in Kumasi, Ghana, and had a lively chat with my wife and I at a time when all the visitors were gone. She gave us some medical insights, and then held my hand to pray with tender compassion. We always recount her prayer as one of the most inspiring and genuinely offered intercessory prayer from the heart to God on our behalf, and I could feel God's Presence as she prayed. The mail is published unedited (verbatim, without alteration of a single word or letter, except that the name has been abbreviated).

Date: Sat, 6 Nov 2010 13:57:54 -0700
From: Dr. N.F.G.
Subject: You are a blessing indeed!
To: Kisseadoo@msn.com

Dear Daddy,
I bless God for granting me the great grace of knowing you at this time of my life.
It's amazing how the LORD has used you to bless me during this challenging period of my life. Indeed it's true when He said that when I pass through the rivers, I will not be overwhelmed and that when I walk through the fire I will not be burned.

It's quite rare to encounter people who genuinely care enough to spare time for you, not to talk about enriching your life with counsel, the word of God and prayer. You, Daddy, are a precious and priceless gem in the vineyard of our LORD and it's my prayer that you will forever remain green like a tree planted by the streams of waters, bearing fruit in and out of season, and prospering in all that you do.

I laugh in my spirit when I think about the fact that such a wonderful life was nearly snuffed out by the devil. Ha! The devil is a liar! You will indeed live to the fullness of your age and you will continue to wax great and greater still. May the LORD grant you peace on every side and may He keep you in the shelter of His Presence, safe and secure from the schemes of men and from accusing tongues.
Thank you for being who you are.

I'll continue to bear you up in my prayers.

Always,
N. F.

==

B) HOW TO BECOME A TRUE CHRISTIAN AND STAY SAVED

These days, many ideas float around about **religion, God,** and **salvation,** and people are seeking after God through several man-made religious pathways. But God has already simplified his method of salvation and specified the only real channel to Himself for us in the Bible — our Lord Jesus Christ. I seriously recommend Jesus to you. It is not just **religion** that we are talking about, but the discussion is about real **LIFE** (connection and fellowship with God Almighty our Creator).

I (Samuel Kisseadoo) gave my heart and life to Jesus Christ when I was 17 years old in High School. My father died when I was 12 years old. I was in church but following friends to do whatever pleased me, and giving my mother heartaches. But when I was confronted with the truth of God's love for me and His punishment for sin, and made to understand that Christ is the only real Savior of mankind who died and shed His Blood to save us all, I became convicted and convinced to give myself to Christ. I then prayed to confess my sins, and honestly accepted Jesus into my heart (soul) by faith. I began reading my Bible and praying daily, and saw tremendous changes in my mind, heart, and life. I even adopted a motto **NBNB (No Bible No Breakfast)** as a guided principle, and tenaciously stuck to it in order to develop a habit of daily Bible reading and meditation. That was in 1969, and up till today, Jesus has been my personal Savior, and has also been Lord over my life as I worship and consult Him in prayer and through the scriptures for wisdom, guidance, and power in all aspects of my life. It is the Lord who has kept me and also kept my wife, and watched over our family in my years of marriage since 1982.

The basic facts you need to understand, and the necessary steps you have to follow are these:

1) I was born in sin, just like everyone else (Romans 3:23). No one is without sin in this world (Ecclesiastes 7:20).

2) No one is righteous on his or her own merits before God (Romans 3:10; Isaiah 64:6).

3) Sin separates me from God, and will land me in hell after death. I also lose God's blessings in this life by having no relationship with God. (Romans 6:23).

4) Every human being will one day stand before God to be judged by Him, and sentenced to Hell, or justified to be in Heaven forever with God (2 Corinthians 5: 10; Revelations 15: 11-15; Romans 2:4-11). We are warned

that one day God will judge all the secrets of men by Jesus Christ (Romans 2:16).

5) God sent His only Son Jesus to come and die for me on the Cross of Calvary. Eternal life is given to us by God the father only through Christ. Jesus is the only one who can redeem me and set me free (Romans 3:23 and Romans 6:23; St. John 3:16; St. John 8:32, 36). Anyone who does not have the Spirit of Jesus does not have life (is dead and spiritually separated from God) – 1 John 5:11-13; Romans 8:9, 14, 16.

6) Becoming a child of God is never automatic for any human being, no matter how good you think you are. You need a special right and power to become a true child of God, and this power is given only by Jesus Christ, when you receive Him into your heart (center of your soul) as your Savior and Lord. *"As many as received Him, to them He gave the right (power) to become children of God, to those who believe in His Name"* (St. John 1:12).

7) Only the Blood of Jesus can deal with my sin nature, wash away my sins, make me clean before a Holy God, justify me, and give me peace within my soul (1 John 1:9; Hebrews 9:22; Romans 5:1).

8) If I confess with my mouth that I was born in sin, repent of my sins, ask Jesus to wash (cleanse) me in His Blood, come to live in me with His Spirit (Holy Spirit), and sincerely believe all of it in my heart, Jesus will faithfully forgive all of my sins and come to reside in my soul for me to become saved (Romans 10:9-13). This is how to be **born again**, and is the only way to be **saved** and become a **true Christian** (St. John 3:3; Acts 4:12; Romans 8:1, 5-8, 9, 14).

9) God does not reject anyone who comes to Him through Jesus Christ (St. John 6:37).

10) I must confess Jesus and pray by faith, and believe that God keeps his promises, and will definitely save me forever (Romans 5:1, 2; Hebrews 11:6; 2 Corinthians 5:7).

11) After being born again, I must grow in the Lord, know him more, and become stronger by reading my Bible and meditating on some scriptures daily, along with daily prayers. I must do my best to obey God's teachings in the Bible by His help. I must therefore practice righteousness, and live in holiness, which will enable me to bear the fruit of the Holy Spirit of God (Galatians 5:22, 23).
I should not just have Jesus as Savior, but surrender all areas of my life to Jesus and make Him Lord over my life as well. I must persistently use His

word and prayer plus God's grace to fortify my willingness to say no to every form of sin, and take steps to overcome all temptations by the power of the Spirit of Jesus within me (Colossians 2:6, 7; 2 Peter 3:18; Ephesians 6:10; 1 Corinthians 10:13).

12) I must become a member of a good Bible–believing church and fellowship of true Christians, where I can fellowship with God's children and enhance my spiritual growth. That will enable me to develop and properly use my talents and gifts to produce fruits that glorify God (Hebrews 10: 23-25; 1 Thessalonians 5:11).

13) I should witness (share my experiences, and let others know about my faith) by my lifestyle, and by telling them about my new life, the great faith, peace, and joy that I have found in Jesus Christ (Mathew 5:16; Acts 5:32; 1 Peter 2:9).

The Lord Jesus wants you not only to be born again, but He has a plan for you to become His disciple (disciplined follower) for the rest of your life. The blessings are incalculable.

I trust that you will carefully consider these points, and act upon them. I pray that the Lord will reveal Himself to you, give you understanding of His love for you, show you more of His ways as you humbly walk with God, and help you to draw close to Him.

I hope to meet you one day, but if we never meet at all on this earth, then please promise me that we shall meet in Heaven.

*"For by **grace** you are **saved** through **faith**; it is not of yourselves; it is the **gift of God**"* (Ephesians 2:8).

"He (God our Savior) is able to keep YOU from falling, and to present YOU faultless before the Presence of his glory with exceeding joy" (Jude 1:24).

"Faithful is He who calls YOU, who also will do it" (1 Thessalonians 5:24).

"The Lord Jesus Christ be with your spirit" (2 Timothy 4:22).

OTHER BOOKS WRITTEN AND PUBLISHED
BY DR KISSEADOO SINCE 2001

1) EFFECTIVE
Publishers call this book a masterpiece.
Different kinds of communication. How to be a good conversationalist.
Importance of communication. How to become an effective communicator etc.

2) FAITH FOR OUR TIMES
Different categories of faith. Weaknesses of Abraham (Father of faith) and lessons we can learn. How to obtain faith and deepen your faith. Faith and healing. Faith versus optimism. Faith and vision etc.

3) CHOOSING A SPOUSE & LIVING A CONTENTED FAMILY LIFE
35 factors to look for before marrying someone; 45 that support the 35; and 50 that support all of them. What is courting, engagement, blessing of marriage. Gift of sex (with information on sexual practices, abortion, in-vitro fertilization, the major birth-control methods and effectiveness, how to satisfy your spouse sexually etc. Divorce and separation. Family ministry. Family finances etc..

4) BASIC PRINCIPLES OF SUCCESSFUL PARENTING
Definition of parenting. The 3 major seasons of parenting. Role of fathers. Discipline. Single parents etc.

5) SPIRITUAL WARFARE
How Lucifer became Satan. 10 reasons why Adam did not divorce Eve. Reasons for intense demonic attacks on marriages and families. Personal testimonies of occult practices the author was exposed to when he was young. How to recognize demonic activities in people's lives. How to cast our demons. Freedom from satanic bondages. The armor of God. Do Juju people really heal diseases? 22 reasons why Nehemiah was able to say 'The Lord will fight for us'. The 4 major categories of demonic activities etc.

6) OVERCOMING YOUR TRIALS AND SUFFERING
The different kinds of trials we face. Personal testimonies. Practical steps to deal effectively with trials and suffering. Value of trials etc.

7) WHY DO WE MARRY, & WHO IS THE HEAD OF THE HOME?
15 main reasons why we marry. Who is really the Head of every home? etc.

8) THE CLIMATE OF PRAYER
This book on prayer won an award at the first National Christian Writers Award in Accra, Ghana, in July 2007 as one of the top 3 prayer books written in Ghana. Dr. Kisseadoo was in Ghana in July 2007 to receive the award at the Accra International Conference Center. A church in Ohio, for example, ordered copies as their main study book on prayer, and other groups have used it too. It details 31reasons why you should pray. What to do when you can't pray. Personal testimonies. Family prayers etc.

9) CONFLICT RESOLUTION & AGREEMENT
Several churches have used this book for Sunday School teaching, and many people have used it for for studies on conflict management. Provides 10 major steps to resolve every kind of conflict. Building of trust as the final step in conflict resolution.

10) TEN KEYS FOR SUCCESS AND PROSPERITY
The 10 primary factors necessary to achieve success and become prosperous in what you do, based on Joshua chapter 1.

11) UNDERSTANDING THE DIFFERENCES BETWEEN MALES AND FEMALES
Analysis of the fundamental differences between males and females — biological, physical, social, sexual etc. How to use these differences to build strong marriages and other relationships.

12) THE NEEDS OF MEN AND WOMEN IN RELATIONSHIPS
15 things men want from women, and 34 things that women want from men for contentment in all marriages and relationships.

13) CHALLENGES OF MODERN MEN AND WOMEN IN RELATIONSHIPS
Present day challenges of sexuality, parenting, finances and property, fashion, technology, long-distance relationships, singleness etc. in our relationships.